Praise for Tobias Wolff and *This Boy's Life*

"His raw works of fiction examine themes of American iden-
tity and individual morality. With wit and compassion, Mr.
Wolff's work reflects the truths of our human experience."
—Barack Obama, National Medals of Arts Ceremony

"A classic of the genre that has lost none of its power . . . His
prose lights up the experience of growing up in America during this era." —Dwight Garner, *New York Times*,
"The 50 Best Memoirs of the Past 50 Years"

"A work of genuine literary art . . . as grim and eerie as *Great
Expectations*, as surreal and cruel as *The Painted Bird*, as comic
and transcendent as *Huckleberry Finn*."
—*Philadelphia Inquirer*

"So absolutely clear and hypnotic . . . that a reader wants to
take it apart and find some simple way to describe why it
works so beautifully." —*New York Times*

"Wolff's genius is in his fine storytelling. *This Boy's Life* reads
and entertains as easily as a novel. Wolff's writing and timing
are superb, as are his depictions of those of us who endured
the '50s." —*The Oregonian*

THIS
BOY'S
LIFE

ALSO BY TOBIAS WOLFF

In the Garden of the North American Martyrs

Back in the World

The Barracks Thief

In Pharaoh's Army

The Night in Question

Old School

Our Story Begins

THIS BOY'S LIFE

A Memoir

30TH ANNIVERSARY EDITION

TOBIAS WOLFF

Grove Press
New York

Published simultaneously in Canada
Printed in the United States of America

THIRTIETH ANNIVERSARY EDITION

First Grove Atlantic hardcover edition: January 1989
This Grove Atlantic edition: December 2019

This book is set in 11.5-point Scala LF
by Alpha Design and Composition of Pittsfield, NH

Library of Congress Cataloging-in-Publication data is available for this title.

ISBN 978-0-8021-4907-7
eISBN 978-0-8021-9860-0

Grove Press
an imprint of Grove Atlantic
154 West 14th Street
New York, NY 10011

Distributed by Publishers Group West

groveatlantic.com

21 22 23 24   10 9 8 7 6 5 4 3 2

For Michael and Patrick

I am especially grateful to my wife, Catherine, for her many careful readings of this book. I would also like to thank Rosemary Hutchins, Geoffrey Wolff, Gary Fisketjon, and Amanda Urban for their help and support. I have been corrected on some points, mostly of chronology. Also my mother thinks that a dog I describe as ugly was actually quite handsome. I've allowed some of these points to stand, because this is a book of memory, and memory has its own story to tell. But I have done my best to make it tell a truthful story.

My first stepfather used to say that what I didn't know would fill a book. Well, here it is.

"The first duty in life is to assume a pose. What the second is, no one has yet discovered."

OSCAR WILDE

"He who fears corruption fears life."

SAUL ALINSKY

Introduction to the 30th Anniversary Edition

I started writing fiction as a schoolboy, imitating the kind of stories I loved to read—stories by O. Henry and Edgar Allen Poe; later, Jack London, and later still Ernest Hemingway. And for many years I remained dedicated to fiction, where I could give myself free rein, drawing on my own experiences as much or as little as I liked, while wrapping them in stories and characters of my own creation. The veil of fiction gave me liberty not only to invent, but also to tell the truth, even deeply personal truth, which is easier to do from behind a mask. Thus you can say what you have to say, confess what you must confess, and at the same time deflect judgment by appealing to fiction's implicit claim that the faults on display are the faults of a *character*, and certainly not—or at least not necessarily—your own. In this way writers of fiction set themselves apart from the fallen creatures whose troubles and shortcomings give shape to their stories, hovering above the fray "like the God of the Creation," as Joyce suggests, "invisible, refined out of existence, indifferent, paring his fingernails."

The memoirist enjoys no such elevation from this human mess, no concealment from its scrutiny, no immunity from its judgments. Though I admired the best of them—Frank Conroy's *Stop-Time*, for example, Mary McCarthy's *Memories of a Catholic Girlhood*, Nabokov's *Speak, Memory*, or my brother Geoffrey's *The Duke of Deception*—I had no wish to write a memoir. I was shy of the personal exposure unavoidable in such a project, and also of the question it posed: Who would care? I was not a famous writer or any kind of famous, and with very few exceptions most memoirs of the time depended for their interest on the celebrity of the writer—Oscar-winning actors, war-winning generals, and so on.

But here it is—the memoir I did not intend to write. Why did I do it, after all? It happened this way, or roughly this way. A colleague of mine came to dinner one night with his wife. In the course of the evening, he made a few references to what he supposed to be our shared background, a background of prosperity and comfort and seamless ascent to our current pampered condition as university professors. His inaccurate assumptions about my history were mildly irritating, but on reflection I couldn't really fault him. I had gone to good schools, lived in a nice house, drove a Volvo, read deep books. He didn't know the particulars of my background, and why should he? Except with my mother and my brother I rarely talked about the past, not out of any shame, but because I was more interested in what was going on in the present with my growing family, my work as a teacher, and scrounging for time to write new stories while fretting over the fate of those I was sending out to various journals and, later, book publishers.

Not long after that dinner with my colleague, I began to write this book. It is almost always a mistake to assign a single cause to changes of heart or mind. Though I've put weight on that conversation, with its good-willed but annoying presumption, it probably just gave a nudge to a possibility I hadn't really dismissed, of writing about my early life with my mother. In any case, I wanted to leave some record of those years for my young children, who, knowing so little of my past, might well have grown up assuming that the privileged life we enjoyed was somehow natural and even inevitable. It was not. I'd been a better prospect for the penitentiary than for the college lectern or the writer's desk. My mother, once so glamorous and unconventional, footloose to the point of recklessness, had settled into respectable retirement in Florida, serving as secretary of the Deltona Lakes Garden Club, and, for a time, president of the League of Women Voters of Volusia County.

Indeed, she had become quite proper and just a little prim, my mother, and her grandchildren could not have seen in her the adventuress who pulled up stakes to drive us across the country almost on a whim, trusting our fortunes to a car that could go barely a hundred miles without boiling over; who had jerked sodas at the Dairy Queen all day to support us and attended secretarial college at night, bootstrapping her way up from job to somewhat better job, for years just a paycheck away from ruin. Through all these moves, all these jobs, all these boarding houses and basement apartments, my mother kept her spirit and hopefulness and sense of humor.

In fact, she had a sort of innocent glow about her that others were quick to note. Not all of those others deserved her trust, and at times her judgment, especially where men were concerned, failed her. Failures of judgment can shape our lives. They shaped mine for years, and they certainly helped shape hers. But so did her natural generosity and appetite for life. She made friends easily, and kept them, as she kept her love of movement and adventure. In her fifties she took a long, entirely unplanned excursion in an open Jeep through remote villages in the Atlas Mountains of Morocco with a companion she'd just met on the flight to Tangiers. In her seventies, and not in the best of health, she considered buying a Winnebago and driving around the country again, but this time alone, as she would never have been able to pry her then-husband off the couch. I was barely able to talk her out of it, and maybe I shouldn't have.

That was the woman I wanted my children to know. At first I told myself that I was writing about my early life with her to leave a sort of informal history for my family, and to create a bank of memories for me to draw on for my fiction. That soon changed. As I wrote I found myself caught up in the past, not simply observing it from a distance, but living it again, vividly. I sometimes had to stop writing, I was so overcome by embarrassment and regret for things I had done; by admiration for my mother's courage, and gratitude for her loyalty; by anger at the cruelty and abuse we both suffered at the hands of a petty, foolish, dangerous man; by laughter at that man's absurdity, and the other absurdities that marked our life together, including those of my own delusions and behavior; and by thankfulness for the profound friendship we had. I put other writings to the side as the project became more and more serious, finally an obsession, and thus devoted myself to what I now had to acknowledge was that book I would never write, a memoir.

I remember the past in terms of stories. That's how I think of it, how I talk about it, and how I've written it here. It's true that life doesn't happen to us in stories, that we make stories out of it, and that in making those stories we can't help but put a personal stamp on them, for better or worse. Think of a Thanksgiving dinner with twenty family members, all telling stories of times past, all loudly, even indignantly, correcting each other. For who wants to hear that in your sister's recollection you are credited with only a cameo—or no role at all—in an event where you remember yourself as the star?

But even allowing for the vagaries of memory, for the various ways different people may interpret the same event, it doesn't follow that the stories we tell from our experience are not to be trusted simply because they are personal. This is especially true at the most basic level—that is, the actuality of the incidents we describe. There is a difference between fact and fiction. I am free to have the narrator of a novel say that he spent time in prison when he did not. You know you're reading fiction; you understand that the novelist is revealing an aspect of the narrator's character. But if I say the same false thing in a memoir, to deceive you about myself, that is a lie. The writer is charged to keep these things straight. I can't write a memoir about my childhood in Auschwitz if I grew up in Switzerland. I can't make the claim—as someone has—that I was raised by wolves when I wasn't.

The events I recount in this book actually happened. I wrote it knowing that it would be read by people who shared or observed these experiences—my mother, my brother, friends, schoolmates—and I was therefore conscious of my memories being examined by theirs. And it turned out that our memories sometimes differed, but usually on questions of chronology or interpretation—what someone was really like, how mean or funny or smart he was, whether she really was a good teacher, why we got into that fight behind the school—and not about whether something happened or did not happen. In those instances where a date needed correcting, I corrected it. Otherwise I tended to trust my own recollections. Why not? Memory doesn't work by committee. Finally, this book is my version of things, partial and subjective as that may be.

Though some of what I describe here was difficult to live through, and difficult to relive, I have never been happier in writing a book—recalling that crazy trip across the country, hearing my beautiful mother's laughter at some ridiculous situation we found ourselves in, remembering the open-heartedness of people we met along the way, on that road and roads still ahead, to feel again the warmth of our friendship and all the other friendships that sustained us through the years. For all this I give thanks—for friendship, for family, for narrow escapes, for good work, for the book you hold in your hands.

Tobias Wolff
November 2018

THIS
BOY'S
LIFE

Fortune

Our car boiled over again just after my mother and I crossed the Continental Divide. While we were waiting for it to cool we heard, from somewhere above us, the bawling of an airhorn. The sound got louder and then a big truck came around the corner and shot past us into the next curve, its trailer shimmying wildly. We stared after it. "Oh, Toby," my mother said, "he's lost his brakes."

The sound of the horn grew distant, then faded in the wind that sighed in the trees all around us.

By the time we got there, quite a few people were standing along the cliff where the truck went over. It had smashed through the guardrails and fallen hundreds of feet through empty space to the river below, where it lay on its back among the boulders. It looked pitifully small. A stream of thick black smoke rose from the cab, feathering out in the wind. My mother asked whether anyone had gone to report the accident. Someone had. We stood with the others at the cliff's edge. Nobody spoke. My mother put her arm around my shoulder.

For the rest of the day she kept looking over at me, touching me, brushing back my hair. I saw that the time was right to make a play for souvenirs. I knew she had no money for them, and I had tried not to ask, but now that her guard was down I couldn't help myself. When we pulled out of Grand Junction I owned a beaded Indian belt, beaded moccasins, and a bronze horse with a removable, tooled-leather saddle.

IT WAS 1955 and we were driving from Florida to Utah, to get away from a man my mother was afraid of and to get rich on uranium. We were going to change our luck.

We'd left Sarasota in the dead of summer, right after my tenth birthday, and headed West under low flickering skies that turned black and exploded and cleared just long enough to leave the air gauzy with steam. We drove through Georgia, Alabama, Tennessee, Kentucky, stopping to cool the engine in towns where people moved with arthritic slowness and spoke in thick, strangled tongues. Idlers with rotten teeth surrounded the car to press peanuts on the pretty Yankee lady and her little boy, arguing among themselves about shortcuts. Women looked up from their flower beds as we drove past, or watched us from their porches, sometimes impassively, sometimes giving us a nod and a flutter of their fans.

Every couple of hours the Nash Rambler boiled over. My mother kept digging into her little grubstake but no mechanic could fix it. All we could do was wait for it to cool, then drive on until it boiled over again. (My mother came to hate this machine so much that not long after we got to Utah she gave it away to a woman she met in a cafeteria.) At night we slept in boggy rooms where headlight beams crawled up and down the walls and mosquitoes sang in our ears, incessant as the tires

4

whining on the highway outside. But none of this bothered me. I was caught up in my mother's freedom, her delight in her freedom, her dream of transformation.

Everything was going to change when we got out West. My mother had been a girl in Beverly Hills, and the life we saw ahead of us was conjured from her memories of California in the days before the Crash. Her father, Daddy as she called him, had been a navy officer and a paper millionaire. They'd lived in a big house with a turret. Just before Daddy lost all his money and all his shanty-Irish relatives' money and got himself transferred overseas, my mother was one of four girls chosen to ride on the Beverly Hills float in the Tournament of Roses. The float's theme was "The End of the Rainbow" and it won that year's prize by acclamation. She met Jackie Coogan. She had her picture taken with Harold Lloyd and Marion Davies, whose movie *The Sailor Man* was filmed on Daddy's ship. When Daddy was at sea she and her mother lived a dream life in which, for days at a time, they played the part of sisters.

And the *cars* my mother told me about as we waited for the Rambler to cool—I should have seen the cars! Daddy drove a Franklin touring car. She'd been courted by a boy who had his own Chrysler convertible with a musical horn. And of course there was the Hernandez family, neighbors who'd moved up from Mexico after finding oil under their cactus ranch. The family was large. When they were expected to appear somewhere together they drove singly in a caravan of identical Pierce-Arrows.

Something like that was supposed to happen to us. People in Utah were getting up poor in the morning and going to bed rich at night. You didn't need to be a mining engineer or a mineralogist. All you needed was a Geiger counter. We were on our way to the uranium fields, where my mother would get a job and keep her eyes open. Once she learned the ropes she'd start prospecting for a claim of her own.

And when she found it she planned to do some serious compensating: for the years of hard work, first as a soda jerk and then as a novice secretary, that had gotten her no farther than flat broke and sometimes not that far. For the breakup of our family five years earlier. For the misery of her long affair with a violent man. She was going to make up for lost time, and I was going to help her.

WE GOT TO Utah the day after the truck went down. We were too late—months too late. Moab and the other mining towns had been overrun. All the motels were full. The locals had rented out their bedrooms and living rooms and garages and were now offering trailer space in their front yards for a hundred dollars a week, which was what my mother could make in a month if she had a job. But there were no jobs, and people were getting ornery. There'd been murders. Prostitutes walked the streets in broad daylight, drunk and bellicose. Geiger counters cost a fortune. Everyone told us to keep going.

My mother thought things over. Finally she bought a poor man's Geiger counter, a black light that was supposed to make uranium trace glow, and we started for Salt Lake City. She figured there must be ore somewhere around there. The fact that nobody else had found any meant that we would have the place pretty much to ourselves. To tide us over she planned to take a job with the Kennecott Mining Company, whose personnel officer had responded to a letter of inquiry she'd sent from Florida some time back. He had warned her against coming, said there was no work in Salt Lake and that his own company was about to go out on strike. But his letter was so friendly! My mother just knew she'd get a job out of him. It was as good as guaranteed.

So we drove on through the desert. As we drove, we sang—Irish ballads, folk songs, big-band blues. I was hooked on "Mood Indigo." Again and again I worldwearily crooned "You ain't been blue, no, no, no" while my mother eyed the temperature gauge and babied the engine. Then my throat dried up on me and left me croaking. I was too excited anyway. Our trail was ending. Burma Shave ads and bullet-riddled mileage signs ticked past. As the numbers on those signs grew smaller we began calling them out at the top of our lungs.

I didn't come to Utah to be the same boy I'd been before. I had my own dreams of transformation, Western dreams, dreams of freedom and dominion and taciturn self-sufficiency. The first thing I wanted to do was change my name. A girl named Toby had joined my class before I left Florida, and this had caused both of us scalding humiliation.

I wanted to call myself Jack, after Jack London. I believed that having his name would charge me with some of the strength and competence inherent in my idea of him. The odds were good that I'd never have to share a classroom with a girl named Jack. And I liked the sound. Jack. Jack Wolff. My mother didn't like it at all, neither the idea of changing my name nor the name itself. I did not drop the subject. She finally agreed, but only on condition that I attend catechism classes. Once I was ready to be received into the Church she would allow me to take Jonathan as my baptismal name and shorten it to Jack. In the meantime I could introduce myself as Jack when I started school that fall.

My father got wind of this and called from Connecticut to demand that I stick to the name he had given me. It was, he said, an old family name. This turned out to be untrue. It just sounded like an old family name, as the furniture he bought at antique stores looked like old family furniture, and as the coat of arms he'd designed for himself looked like the shield of some fierce baron who'd spent his life wallowing in Saracen gore, charging from battle to battle down muddy roads lined with groveling peasants and churls.

He was also unhappy about my becoming a Catholic. "My family," he told me, "has always been Protestant. Episcopalian, actually." Actually, his family had always been Jews, but I had to wait another ten years before learning this. In the extremity of his displeasure my father even put my older brother on the phone. I was surly, and Geoffrey didn't really care what I called myself, and there it ended.

My mother was pleased by my father's show of irritation and stuck up for me. A new name began to seem like a good idea to her. After all, he was in Connecticut and we were in Utah. Though my father was rolling in money at the time—he had married the millionairess he'd been living with before the divorce—he sent us nothing, not even the pittance the judge had prescribed for my support. We were barely making it, and making it in spite of him. My shedding the name he'd given me would put him in mind of that fact.

That fall, once a week after school, I went to catechism. Yellow leaves drifted past the windows as Sister James instructed us in the life of faith. She was a woman of passion. Her square jaw trembled when something moved her, and as she talked her eyes grew brilliant behind her winking rimless glasses. She could not sit still. Instead she paced between our desks, her habit rustling against us. She had no timidity or coyness. Even about sex she spoke graphically and with gusto. Sometimes she would forget where she was and start whistling.

Sister James did not like the idea of us running free after school. She feared we would spend our time with friends from the public schools we attended and possibly end up as Mormons. To account for our afternoons she had formed the Archery Club, the Painting Club, and the Chess Club, and she demanded that each of us join one. They met twice a week. Attendance was compulsory. No one thought of disobeying her.

I belonged to the Archery Club. Girls were free to join but none did. On rainy days we practiced in the church basement, on clear days outside. Sister James watched us when she could; at other times we were supervised by an older nun who was nearsighted and tried to control us by saying, "Boys, boys . . ."

The people next door kept cats. The cats were used to having the run of the churchyard and it took them a while to understand that they were no longer predators but prey—big calicoes and marmalades sitting in the sunshine, tails curled prettily around themselves, cocking their heads from side to side as our arrows zipped past. We never hit any of them, but we came close. Finally the cats caught on and quit the field. When this happened we began hunting each other.

Pretending to look for overshot arrows, we would drift beyond the targets to a stand of trees where the old nun couldn't see us. There the game began. At first the idea was to creep around and let fly in such a way that your arrow thunked into the tree nearest your quarry. For a time we were content to count this a hit. But the rule proved too confining for some, and then the rest of us had no choice but to throw it over too, as friends of mine would later throw over the rules governing fights with water balloons, rocks, and BB guns.

The game got interesting. All of us had close calls, close calls that were recounted until they became legend. The Time Donny Got Hit in the Wallet. The Time Patrick Had His Shoe Shot Off. A few of the boys came to their senses and dropped out but the rest of us carried on. We did so in a resolutely innocent way, never admitting to ourselves what the real object was: that is, to bring somebody down. Among the trees I achieved absolute vacancy of mind. I had no thought of being hurt or of hurting anyone else, not even as I notched my arrow and pulled it back, intent on some movement in the shadows ahead. I was doing just that one afternoon, drawing my bow, ready to fire as soon as my target showed himself again, when I heard a rustling behind me. I spun around.

Sister James had been about to say something. Her mouth was open. She looked at the arrow I was aiming at her, then looked at me. In her presence my thoughtlessness forsook me. I knew exactly what I had been doing. We stood like that for a time. Finally I pointed the arrow at the ground. I unnotched it and started to make some excuse, but she closed her eyes at the sound of my voice and waved her hands as if to shoo away gnats. "Practice is over," she said. Then she turned and left me there.

*   *   *

I WAS SUBJECT to fits of feeling myself unworthy, somehow deeply at fault. It didn't take much to bring this sensation to life, along with the certainty that everybody but my mother saw through me and did not like what they saw. There was no reason for me to have this feeling. I thought I'd left it back in Florida, together with my fear of fighting and my shyness with girls, but here it was, come to meet me.

Sister James had nothing to do with it. She hated talking about sin, and was plainly bored by our obsessive questions about Hell and Purgatory and Limbo. The business with the arrow probably meant nothing to her. To her I was just another boy doing some dumb boyish thing. But I began to feel that she knew all about me, and that a good part of her life was now given over to considering how bad I was.

I became furtive around her. I began skipping archery and even some of my catechism classes. There was no immediate way for my mother to find out. We didn't have a telephone and she never went to church. She thought it was good for me but beside the point for herself, especially now that she was divorced and once again involved with Roy, the man she'd left Florida to get away from.

When I could, I ran around with boys from school. But they all came from Mormon families. When they weren't being instructed in their own faith, which was a lot of the time, their parents liked to have them close by. Most afternoons I wandered around in the trance that habitual solitude induces. I walked downtown and stared at merchandise. I imagined being adopted by different people I saw on the street. Sometimes, seeing a man in a suit come toward me from a distance that blurred his features, I would prepare myself to recognize my father and to be recognized by him. Then we would pass each other and a few minutes later I would pick someone else. I talked to anyone who would talk back. When the need came upon me, I knocked on the door of the nearest house and asked to use the bathroom. No one ever refused. I sat in other people's yards and played with their dogs. The dogs got to know me—by the end of the year they'd be waiting for me.

I also wrote long letters to my pen pal in Phoenix, Arizona. Her name was Alice. My class had been exchanging letters with her class since school began. We were supposed to write once a month but I wrote at least once a week, ten, twelve, fifteen pages at a time. I represented myself to her as the owner of a palomino horse named Smiley who shared my encounters with mountain lions, rattlesnakes, and packs of coyotes on my father's ranch, the Lazy B. When I wasn't busy on the ranch I raised German shepherds and played for several athletic teams. Although Alice was a terse and irregular correspondent, I believed that she must be in awe of me, and imagined someday presenting myself at her door to claim her adoration.

So I passed the hours after school. Sometimes, not very often, I felt lonely. Then I would go home to Roy.

ROY HAD TRACKED us down to Salt Lake a few weeks after we arrived. He took a room somewhere across town but spent most of his time in our apartment, making it clear that he would hold no grudges as long as my mother walked the line.

Roy didn't work. He had a small inheritance and supplemented that with disability checks from the VA, which he claimed he would lose if he took a job. When he wasn't hunting or fishing or checking up on my mother, he sat at the kitchen table with a cigarette in his mouth and squinted at *The Shooter's Bible* through the smoke that veiled his face. He always seemed glad to see me. If I was lucky he would put a couple of rifles in his Jeep and we'd drive into the desert to shoot at cans and look for ore. He'd caught the uranium bug from my mother.

Roy rarely spoke on these trips. Every so often he would look at me and smile, then look away again. He seemed always deep in thought, staring at the road through mirrored sunglasses, the wind ruffling the perfect waves of his hair. Roy was handsome in the conventional way that appeals to boys. He had a tattoo. He'd been to war and kept a kind of silence about it that was full of heroic implication. He was graceful in his movements. He could fix the Jeep if he had to, though he preferred to drive halfway across Utah to a mechanic he'd heard about from some loudmouth in a bar. He was an expert hunter who always got his buck. He taught both my mother and me to shoot, taught my mother so well that she became a better shot than he was—a real deadeye.

My mother didn't tell me what went on between her and Roy, the threats and occasional brutality with which he held her in place. She was the same as ever with me, full of schemes and quick to laugh. Only now and then there came a night when she couldn't do anything but sit and cry, and then I comforted her, but I never knew her reasons. When these nights were over I put them from my mind. If there were other signs, I didn't see them. Roy's strangeness and the strangeness of our life with him had, over the years, become ordinary to me.

I thought Roy was what a man should be. My mother must have thought so too, once. I believed that I should like him, and pretended to myself that I did like him, even to the point of seeking out his company. He turned on me just one time. I had discovered that my mother's cooking oil glowed like phosphorus under the black light, the way uranium was supposed to, and one day I splashed it all over some rocks we'd brought in. Roy got pretty worked up when he looked at them. I had to tell him why I was laughing so hard, and he didn't take it well. He gave me a hard, mean look. He stood there for a while, just holding me with this look, and finally he said, "That's not funny," and didn't speak to me again the rest of the night.

On our way back from the desert Roy would park near the insurance company where my mother, after learning that Kennecott really was out on strike, had found work as a secretary. He waited outside until she got off work. Then he followed her home, idling along the road, here and there pulling into a driveway to let her get ahead, then pulling out again to keep her in sight. If my mother had ever glanced behind her she would have spotted the Jeep immediately. But she didn't. She walked along in her crisp military stride, shoulders braced, head erect, and never looked back. Roy acted as though this were a game we were all playing. I knew it wasn't a game but I didn't know what it was, so I kept the promises he extracted from me to say nothing to her.

One afternoon near Christmas we missed her. She was not among the people who left when the building closed. Roy waited for a while, peering up at the darkened windows, watching the guard lock the doors. Then he panicked. He threw the Jeep into gear and sped around the block. He stopped in front of the building again. He turned off the engine and began whispering to himself. "Yes," he said, "okay, okay," and turned the engine back on. He drove around the block one more time and then tore down the neighboring streets, alternately slamming on the brakes and gunning the engine, his cheeks wet with tears, his lips moving like a supplicant's. This had all happened before, in Sarasota, and I knew better than to say anything. I just held onto the passenger grip and tried to look normal.

Finally he came to a stop. We sat there for a few minutes. When he seemed better I asked if we could go home. He nodded without looking at me, then took a handkerchief from his shirt pocket, blew his nose, and put the handkerchief away.

My mother was cooking dinner and listening to carols when we came in. The windows were all steamed up. Roy watched me go over to the stove and lean against her. He kept looking at me until I looked at him. Then he winked. I knew he wanted me to wink back, and I also knew that it would somehow put me on his side if I did.

My mother hung one arm around my shoulders while she stirred the sauce. A glass of beer stood on the counter next to her.

"So how was archery?" she asked.

"Okay," I said. "Fine."

Roy said, "We went out afterwards and shot a few bottles. Then we went tomcatting."

"Tomcatting," my mother repeated coldly. She hated the word.

Roy leaned against the refrigerator. "Busy day?"

"Real busy. Hectic."

"Not a minute to spare, huh?"

"They kept us hopping," she said. She took a sip of beer and licked her lips.

"Must've been good to get out."

"It was. Real good."

"Terrific," Roy said. "Have a nice walk home?"

She nodded.

Roy smiled at me, and I gave in. I smiled back.

"I don't know who you think you're fooling," Roy said to her. "Even your own kid knows what you're up to." He turned and walked back into the living room. My mother closed her eyes, then opened them again and went on stirring.

It was one of those dinners where we didn't talk. Afterward my mother got out her typewriter. She had lied about her typing speed in order to get work, and now her boss expected more from her than she could really do. That meant having to finish at night the reports she couldn't get through

at the office. While she typed, Roy glowered at her over the
the rifles he was cleaning and I wrote a letter to Alice. I put
the letter in an envelope and gave it to my mother to mail.
Then I went to bed.

Late that night I woke up and heard Roy's special nag-
ging murmur, the different words blurring into one continuous sound through the wall that separated us. It seemed to
go on and on. Then I heard my mother say, *Shopping!* I was
shopping! Can't I go shopping? Roy resumed his murmur.
I lay there, hugging the stuffed bear I was too old for and
had promised to give up when I officially got my new name.
Moonlight filled my room, an unheated addition at the rear
of the apartment. On bright cold nights like this one I could
see the cloud of my breath and pretend that I was smoking,
as I did now until I fell asleep again.

I WAS BAPTIZED during Easter along with several others from
my catechism class. To prepare ourselves for communion we
were supposed to make a confession, and Sister James ap-
pointed a time that week for each of us to come to the rectory
and be escorted by her to the confessional. She would wait
outside until we were finished and then guide us through
our penance.

I thought about what to confess, but I could not break
my sense of being at fault down to its components. Trying to
get a particular sin out of it was like fishing a swamp, where
you feel the tug of something that at first seems promising

and then resistant and finally hopeless as you realize that you've snagged the bottom, that you have the whole planet on the other end of your line. Nothing came to mind. I didn't see how I could go through with it, but in the end I hauled myself down to the church and kept my appointment. To have skipped it would have called attention to all my other absences and possibly provoked a visit from Sister James to my mother. I couldn't risk having the two of them compare notes.

Sister James met me as I was coming into the rectory. She asked if I was ready and I said I guessed so.

"It won't hurt," she said. "No more than a shot, anyway."

We walked over to the church and down the side aisle to the confessional. Sister James opened the door for me. "In you go," she said. "Make a good one now."

I knelt with my face to the screen as we had been told to do and said, "Bless me Father for I have sinned."

I could hear someone breathing loudly on the other side. After a time he said, "Well?"

I folded my hands together and closed my eyes and waited for something to present itself.

"You seem to be having some trouble." His voice was deep and scratchy.

"Yes sir."

"Call me Father. I'm a priest, not a gentleman. Now then, you understand that whatever gets said in here stays in here."

"Yes Father."

"I suppose you've thought a lot about this. Is that right?"

I said that I had.

"Well, you've just given yourself a case of nerves, that's all. How about if we try again a little later. Shall we do that?"

"Yes please, Father."

"That's what we'll do, then. Just wait outside a second."

I stood and left the confessional. Sister James came toward me from where she'd been standing against the wall. "That wasn't so bad now, was it?" she asked.

"I'm supposed to wait," I told her.

She looked at me. I could see she was curious, but she didn't ask any questions.

The priest came out soon after. He was old and very tall and walked with a limp. He stood close beside me, and when I looked up at him I saw the white hair in his nostrils. He smelled strongly of tobacco. "We had a little trouble getting started," he said.

"Yes, Father?"

"He's just a bit nervous is all," the priest said. "Needs to relax. Nothing like a glass of milk for that."

She nodded.

"Why don't we try again a little later. Say twenty minutes?"

"We'll be here, Father."

Sister James and I went to the rectory kitchen. I sat at a steel cutting table while she poured me a glass of milk. "You want some cookies?" she asked.

"That's all right, Sister."

"Sure you do." She put a package of Oreos on a plate and brought it to me. Then she sat down. With her arms crossed, hands hidden in her sleeves, she watched me eat and drink. Finally she said, "What happened, then? Cat get your tongue?"

"Yes, Sister."

"There's nothing to be afraid of."

"I know."

"Maybe you're just thinking of it wrong," she said.

I stared at my hands on the tabletop.

"I forgot to give you a napkin," she said. "Go on and lick them. Don't be shy."

She waited until I looked up, and when I did I saw that she was younger than I'd thought her to be. Not that I'd given much thought to her age. Except for the really old nuns with canes or facial hair they all seemed outside of time, without past or future. But now—forced to look at Sister James across the narrow space of this gleaming table—I saw her differently. I saw an anxious woman of about my mother's age who wanted to help me without knowing what kind of help I needed. Her good will worked strongly on me. My eyes burned and my throat swelled up. I would have surrendered to her if only I'd known how.

"It probably isn't as bad as you think it is," Sister James said. "Whatever it is, someday you'll look back and you'll see that it was natural. But you've got to bring it to the light. Keeping it in the dark is what makes it feel so bad." She added, "I'm not asking you to tell me, understand. That's not my place. I'm just saying that we all go through these things."

Sister James leaned forward over the table. "When I was your age," she said, "maybe even a little older, I used to go through my father's wallet while he was taking his bath at night. I didn't take bills, just pennies and nickels, maybe a dime. Nothing he'd miss. My father would've given me the money if I'd asked for it. But I preferred to steal it. Stealing from him made me feel awful, but I did it all the same."

She looked down at the tabletop. "I was a backbiter, too. Whenever I was with one friend I would say terrible things about my other friends, and then turn around and do the same thing to the one I had just been with. I knew what I was doing, too. I hated myself for it, I really did, but that didn't stop me. I used to wish that my mother and my brothers would die in a car crash so I could grow up with just my father and have everyone feel sorry for me."

Sister James shook her head. "I had all these bad thoughts I didn't want to let go of. Know what I mean?"

I nodded, and presented her with an expression that was meant to register dawning comprehension.

"Good!" she said. She slapped her palms down on the table. "Ready to try again?"

I said that I was.

Sister James led me back to the confessional. I knelt and began again: "Bless me Father, for—"

"All right," he said. "We've been here before. Just talk plain."

"Yes Father."

Again I closed my eyes over my folded hands.

"Come come," he said, with a certain sharpness.

"Yes, Father." I bent close to the screen and whispered, "Father, I steal."

He was silent for a moment. Then he said, "What do you steal?"

"I steal money, Father. From my mother's purse when she's in the shower."

"How long have you been doing this?"

I didn't answer.

"Well?" he said. "A week? A year? Two years?"

I chose the one in the middle. "A year."

"A year," he repeated. "That won't do. You have to stop. Do you intend to stop?"

"Yes, Father."

"Honestly, now."

"Honestly, Father."

"All right. Good. What else?"

"I'm a backbiter."

"A backbiter?"

"I say things about my friends when they're not around."

"That won't do either," he said.

"No, Father."

"That certainly won't do. Your friends will desert you if you persist in this and let me tell you, a life without friends is no life at all."

"Yes, Father."

"Do you sincerely intend to stop?"

"Yes, Father."

"Good. Be sure that you do. I tell you this in all seriousness. Anything else?"

"I have bad thoughts, Father."

"Yes. Well," he said, "why don't we save those for next time. You have enough to work on."

The priest gave me my penance and absolved me. As I left the confessional I heard his own door open and close. Sister James came forward to meet me again, and we waited together as the priest made his way to where we stood. Breathing hoarsely, he steadied himself against a pillar. He laid his other hand on my shoulder. "That was fine," he said. "Just fine." He gave my shoulder a squeeze. "You have a fine boy here, Sister James."

She smiled. "So I do, Father. So I do."

J ust after Easter Roy gave me the Winchester .22 rifle I'd
learned to shoot with. It was a light, pump-action, beautifully balanced piece with a walnut stock black from all its
oilings. Roy had carried it when he was a boy and it was still
as good as new. Better than new. The action was silky from
long use, and the wood of a quality no longer to be found.

The gift did not come as a surprise. Roy was stingy, and
slow to take a hint, but I'd put him under siege. I had my
heart set on that rifle. A weapon was the first condition of
self-sufficiency, and of being a real Westerner, and of all ac-
ceptable employment— trapping, riding herd, soldiering, law
enforcement, and outlawry. I needed that rifle, for itself and
for the way it completed me when I held it.

My mother said I couldn't have it. Absolutely not. Roy
took the rifle back but promised me he'd bring her around. He
could not imagine anyone refusing him anything and treated
the refusals he did encounter as perverse and insincere. Normally mute, he became at these times a relentless whiner. He
would follow my mother from room to room, emitting one
ceaseless note of complaint that was pitched perfectly to jelly
her nerves and bring her to a state where she would agree to
anything to make it stop.

After a few days of this my mother caved in. She said I could have the rifle if, and only if, I promised never to take it out or even touch it except when she and Roy were with me. Okay, I said. Sure. Naturally. But even then she wasn't satisfied. She plain didn't like the fact of me owning a rifle. Roy said he had owned several rifles by the time he was my age, but this did not reassure her. She didn't think I could be trusted with it. Roy said now was the time to find out.

For a week or so I kept my promises. But now that the weather had turned warm Roy was usually off somewhere, and eventually, in the dead hours after school when I found myself alone in the apartment, I decided that there couldn't be any harm in taking the rifle out to clean it. Only to clean it, nothing more. I was sure it would be enough just to break it down, oil it, rub linseed into the stock, polish the octagonal barrel and then hold it up to the light to confirm the perfection of the bore. But it wasn't enough. From cleaning the rifle I went to marching around the apartment with it, and then to striking brave poses in front of the mirror. Roy had saved one of his army uniforms and I sometimes dressed up in this, together with martial-looking articles of hunting gear: fur trooper's hat, camouflage coat, boots that reached nearly to my knees.

The camouflage coat made me feel like a sniper, and before long I began to act like one. I set up a nest on the couch by the front window. I drew the shades to darken the apartment, and took up my position. Nudging the shade aside with the rifle barrel, I followed people in my sights as they walked or drove along the street. At first I made shooting sounds—kyoo! kyoo! Then I started cocking the hammer and letting it snap down.

Roy stored his ammunition in a metal box he kept hidden in the closet. As with everything else hidden in the apartment, I knew exactly where to find it. There was a layer of loose .22 rounds on the bottom of the box under shells of bigger caliber, dropped there by the handful the way men drop pennies on their dressers at night. I took some and put them in a hiding place of my own. With these I started loading up the rifle. Hammer cocked, a round in the chamber, finger resting lightly on the trigger, I drew a bead on whoever walked by—women pushing strollers, children, garbage collectors laughing and calling to each other, anyone—and as they passed under my window I sometimes had to bite my lip to keep from laughing in the ecstasy of my power over them, and at their absurd and innocent belief that they were safe.

But over time the innocence I laughed at began to irritate me. It was a peculiar kind of irritation. I saw it years later in men I served with, and felt it myself, when unarmed Vietnamese civilians talked back to us while we were herding them around. Power can be enjoyed only when it is recognized and feared. Fearlessness in those without power is maddening to those who have it.

One afternoon I pulled the trigger. I had been aiming at two old people, a man and a woman, who walked so slowly that by the time they turned the corner at the bottom of the hill my little store of self-control was exhausted. I had to shoot. I looked up and down the street. It was empty. Nothing moved but a pair of squirrels chasing each other back and forth on the telephone wires. I followed one in my sights. Finally it stopped for a moment and I fired. The squirrel dropped straight into the road. I pulled back into the shadows and waited for something to happen, sure that someone must have heard the shot or seen the squirrel fall. But the sound that was so loud to me probably seemed to our neighbors no more than the bang of a cupboard slammed shut. After a while I sneaked a glance into the street. The squirrel hadn't moved. It looked like a scarf someone had dropped.

When my mother got home from work I told her there was a dead squirrel in the street. Like me, she was an animal lover. She took a cellophane bag off a loaf of bread and we went outside and looked at the squirrel. "Poor little thing," she said. She stuck her hand in the wrapper and picked up the squirrel, then pulled the bag inside out away from her hand. We buried it behind our building under a cross made of popsicle sticks, and I blubbered the whole time.

I blubbered again in bed that night. At last I got out of bed and knelt down and did an imitation of somebody praying, and then I did an imitation of somebody receiving divine reassurance and inspiration. I stopped crying. I smiled to myself and forced a feeling of warmth into my chest. Then I climbed back in bed and looked up at the ceiling with a blissful expression until I went to sleep.

For several days I stayed away from the apartment at times when I knew I'd be alone there. I resumed my old patrol around the city or fooled around with my Mormon friends. One of these was a boy who'd caught everyone's notice on the first day of school by yelling, when a classmate named Boone had his name read out, "Hey!—any relation to Daniel?" His own name was called soon after, and this turned out to be Crockett. He seemed puzzled by the hoots of laughter that followed. Not angry, just puzzled. His father was a jocular man who liked children and used to take mobs of us swimming at the Y and to youth concerts given by the Tabernacle Choir. Mr. Crockett later became a justice of the state supreme court, the same one that granted Gary Gilmore his wish to die.

Though I avoided the apartment, I could not shake the idea that sooner or later I would get the rifle out again. All my images of myself as I wished to be were images of myself armed. Because I did not know who I was, any image of myself, no matter how grotesque, had power over me. This much I understand now. But the man can give no help to the boy, not in this matter nor in those that follow. The boy moves always out of reach.

One afternoon I walked a friend of mine to his house. After he went inside I sat on his steps for a while, then got to my feet and started toward home, walking fast. The apartment was empty. I took the rifle out and cleaned it. Put it back. Ate a sandwich. Took the rifle out again. Though I didn't load it, I did turn the lights off and pull down the shades and assume my position on the couch.

I stayed away for several days after that. Then I came back again. For an hour or so I aimed at people passing by.

Again I teased myself by leaving the rifle unloaded, snapping the hammer on air, trying my own patience like a loose tooth. I had just followed a car out of sight when another car turned the corner at the bottom of the hill. I zeroed in on it, then lowered the rifle. I don't know whether I had ever seen this particular car before, but it was of a type and color—big, plain, blue—usually driven only by government workers and nuns. You could tell if it was nuns by the way their headgear filled the windows and by the way they drove, which was very slowly and anxiously. Even from a distance you could feel the tension radiating from a car full of nuns.

The car crept up the hill. It moved even slower as it approached my building, and then it stopped. The front door on the passenger side opened and Sister James got out. I drew back from the window. When I looked out again, the car was still there but Sister James was not. I knew that the apartment door was locked—I always locked it when I took the rifle out—but I went over and double-checked it anyway. I heard her coming up the steps. She was whistling. She stopped outside the door and knocked. It was an imperative knock. She continued to whistle as she waited. She knocked again.

I stayed where I was, still and silent, rifle in hand, afraid that Sister James would somehow pass through the locked door and discover me. What would she think? What would she make of the rifle, the fur hat, the uniform, the darkened room? What would she make of me? I feared her disapproval, but even more than that I feared her incomprehension, even her amusement, at what she could not possibly understand. I didn't understand it myself. Being so close to so much robust identity made me feel the poverty of my own, the ludicrous aspect of my costume and props. I didn't want to let her in. At the same time, strangely, I did.

After a few moments of this an envelope slid under the door and I heard Sister James going back down the steps. I went to the window and saw her bend low to enter the car, lifting her habit with one hand and reaching inside with the other. She arranged herself on the seat, closed the door, and the car started slowly up the hill. I never saw her again.

The envelope was addressed to Mrs. Wolff. I tore it open and read the note. Sister James wanted my mother to call her. I burned the envelope and note in the sink and washed the ashes down the drain.

Roy was tying flies at the kitchen table. I was drinking a Pepsi and watching him. He bent close to his work, grunting with concentration. He said, in an offhand way, "What do you think about a little brother?"

"A little brother?"

He nodded. "Me and your mom've been thinking about starting a family."

I didn't like this idea at all, in fact it froze me solid.

He looked up from the vise. "We're already pretty much of a family when you think about it," he said.

I said I guessed we were.

"We have a lot of fun." He looked down at the vise again. "A lot of fun. We're thinking about it," he said. "Nothing like a little guy around the house. You could teach him things. You could teach him to shoot."

I nodded.

"That's what we were thinking too," he said. "I don't know about names, though. What do you think of Bill as a name?"

I said I liked it.

"Bill," Roy said. "Bill. Bill." He turned silent again, staring down at the fly in the vise, his hands on the table. I finished off my Pepsi and went outside.

While my mother and I ate breakfast the next morning Roy carried fishing gear and camping equipment out to the Jeep. He was lashing down something in back when I left for school. I yelled "Good luck!" and he waved at me, and I never saw him again either. My mother was in the apartment when I got home that day, folding clothes into a suitcase that lay open on her bed. Two other suitcases were already packed full. She was singing to herself. Her color was high, her movements quick and sure, everything about her flushed with gaiety. I knew we were on our way the moment I heard her voice, even before I saw the suitcases.

She asked me why I wasn't at archery. There was no suspicion behind the question.

"They canceled it," I told her.

"Great," she said. "Now I won't have to go looking for you. Why don't you check your room and make sure I've got everything."

"We going somewhere?"

"Yes." She smoothed out a dress. "We sure are."

"Where?"

She laughed. "I don't know. Any suggestions?"

"Phoenix," I said immediately.

She didn't ask why. She hung the dress in a garment bag and said, "That's a real coincidence, because I was thinking about Phoenix myself. I even got the Phoenix paper. They have lots of opportunities there. Seattle too. What do you think about Seattle?"

I sat down on the bed. It was starting to take hold of me too, the giddiness of flight. My knees shook and I felt myself grin. Everything was racing. I said, "What about Roy?"

She kept on packing. "What about him?"

"I don't know. Is he coming too?"

"Not if I can help it, he isn't." She said she hoped that was okay with me.

I didn't answer. I was afraid of saying something she would remember if they got back together. But I was glad to be once more on the run and glad that I would have her to myself again.

"I know you two are close," she said.

"Not that close."

She said there wasn't time to explain everything now, but later on she would. She tried to sound serious, but she was close to laughing and so was I.

"Better check your room," my mother said again.

"When are we leaving?"

"Right away. As soon as we can."

I ate a bowl of soup while my mother finished packing. She carried the suitcases into the front hall and then walked down to the corner to call a cab. That was when I remembered the rifle. I went to the closet and saw it there with Roy's things, his boots and jackets and ammo boxes. I carried the rifle to the living room and waited for my mother to come back.

"That thing stays," she said when she saw it.

"It's mine," I said.

"Don't make a scene," she told me. "I've had enough of those things. I'm sick of them. Now put it back."

"It's mine," I repeated. "He gave it to me."

"No. I'm sick of guns."

"Mom, it's *mine.*"

She looked out the window. "No. We don't have room for it."

This was a mistake. She had put the argument in practical terms and now it would be impossible for her to argue from principle again. "Look," I said, "There's room. See, I can break it down." And before she could stop me I had unscrewed the locking bolt and pulled the rifle apart. I dragged one of the suitcases back into the living room and unzipped it and slid the two halves of the rifle in between the clothes. "See?" I said. "There's plenty of room."

She had watched all this with her arms crossed, her lips pressed tightly together. She turned to the window again. "Keep it then," she said. "If it means that much to you."

IT WAS RAINING when our cab pulled up. The cabby honked and my mother started wrestling one of the suitcases down the steps. The cabby saw her and got out to help, a big man in a fancy Western shirt that got soaked in the drizzle. He went back for the other two bags while we waited in the cab. My mother kidded him about how wet he was and he kidded her back, looking in the rear-view mirror constantly as if to make sure she was still there. As we approached the Greyhound station he stopped joking and began to quiz her in a low, hurried voice, asking one question after another, and when I got out of the cab he pulled the door shut behind me, leaving the two of them alone inside. Through the rain streaming down the window I could see him talking, talking, and my mother smiling and shaking her head. Then they both got out and he took our bags from the trunk. "You're sure, now?" he said to her. She nodded. When she tried to pay him he said that her money was no good, not to him it wasn't, but she held it out again and he took it.

My mother broke out laughing after he drove away. "Of all things," she said. She kept laughing to herself as we hauled the bags inside, where she settled me on a bench and went to the ticket window. The station was empty except for a family of Indians. All of them, even the children, looked straight ahead and said nothing. A few minutes later my mother came back with our tickets. The Phoenix bus had left already and the next one didn't come through until late that night, but we were in luck—there was a bus leaving for Portland in a couple of hours, and from there we could make an easy connection to Seattle. I tried to conceal my disappointment but my mother saw it and bought me off with a handful of change. I played the pinball machines for a while and then stocked up on candy bars for the trip, Milk Duds and Sugar Babies and Idaho Spuds, most of which were already curdling in my stomach when at dusk we boarded our bus and stood in the dazed regard of the other passengers. We hesitated for a moment as if we might get off. Then my mother took my hand and we made our way down the aisle, nodding to anyone who looked at us, smiling to show we meant well.

Uncool

We lived in a boardinghouse in West Seattle. At night, if my mother wasn't too tired, we took walks around the neighborhood, stopping in front of different houses to consider them as candidates for future purchase. We went for the biggest and most pretentious, sneering at ranches and duplexes—anything that smelled of economy. We chose half-timbered houses, houses with columns, houses with sculpted bushes in front. Then we went back to our room, where I read novels about heroic collies while my mother practiced typing and shorthand so she wouldn't fall behind in her new job.

Our room was in a converted attic. It had two camp beds and between them, under the window, a desk and chair. It smelled of mildew. The yellow wallpaper was new but badly hung and already curling at the edges. It was the kind of room that B-movie detectives wake up in, bound and gagged, after they've been slipped a Mickey.

The boardinghouse was full of old men and men who probably only seemed old. Besides my mother only two women lived there. One was a secretary named Kathy. Kathy was young and plain and shy. She stayed in her room most of the time. When people addressed her she would look at them with a drowning expression, then softly ask them to repeat what they had said. As time went on, her pregnancy began to show through the loose clothes she wore. There didn't seem to be a man in the picture.

The other woman was Marian, the housekeeper. Marian was big and loud. Her arms were as thick as a man's, and when she pounded out hamburger patties the whole kitchen shook. Marian went with a marine sergeant from Bremerton who was even bigger than she was but more gentle and soft-spoken. He had been in the Pacific during the war. When I kept after him to tell me about it he finally showed me an album of photographs he'd taken. Most of the pictures were of his buddies. Doc, a man with glasses. Curly, a man with no hair. Jesus, a man with a beard. But there were also pictures of corpses. He meant to scare me off the subject with these pictures but instead they made me more interested. Finally Marian told me to stop bothering him.

Marian and I disliked each other. Later we both found reasons for it, but our dislike was instinctive and mysterious. I tried to cover mine with a treacly stream of yes ma'ams and no ma'ams and offers of help. Marian wasn't fooled. She knew I didn't like her, and that I was not the young gentleman I pretended to be. She went out a lot, running errands, and she sometimes saw me on the street with my friends—bad company, from the looks of them. She knew I combed my hair differently after I left the house and rearranged my clothes. Once, driving past us, she yelled at me to pull up my pants.

*　　*　　*

MY FRIENDS WERE Terry Taylor and Terry Silver. All three of us lived with our mothers. Terry Taylor's father was stationed in Korea. The war had been over for two years but he still hadn't come home. Mrs. Taylor had filled the house with pictures of him, graduation portraits, snapshots in and out of uniform—always alone, leaning against trees, standing in front of houses. The living room was like a shrine; if you didn't know better you would have thought that he had not survived Korea but had died some kind of hero's death there, as Mrs. Taylor had perhaps anticipated.

This sepulchral atmosphere owed a lot to the presence of Mrs. Taylor herself. She was a tall, stooped woman with deep-set eyes. She sat in her living room all day long and chain-smoked cigarettes and stared out the picture window with an air of unutterable sadness, as if she knew things beyond mortal bearing. Sometimes she would call Taylor over and wrap her long arms around him, then close her eyes and hoarsely whisper, "Terence! Terence!" Eyes still closed, she would turn her head and resolutely push him away.

Silver and I immediately saw the potential of this scene and we replayed it often, so often that we could bring tears to Taylor's eyes just by saying "Terence! Terence!" Taylor was a dreamy thin-skinned boy who cried easily, a weakness from which he tried to distract us by committing acts of ferocious vandalism. He'd once been to juvenile court for breaking windows.

Mrs. Taylor also had two daughters, both older than Terry and full of scorn for us and all our works. "Oh, *God*," they'd say when they saw us. "Look what the cat dragged in." Silver and I suffered their insults meekly, but Taylor always had an answer. "Does your face hurt?" he would say. "I just wondered, it's killing me." "Is that sweater made of camel's hair? I just wondered, I thought I saw two humps."

But they always had the last word. As girls went they were nothing special, but they were girls, and empowered by that fact to render judgment on us. They could make us cringe just by rolling their eyes. Silver and I were afraid of them, and confused by Mrs. Taylor and the funereal atmosphere of the house. The only reason we went there was to steal Mrs. Taylor's cigarettes.

We couldn't go to my place. Phil, the man who owned the boardinghouse, had no use for kids. He rented the room to my mother only after she promised that I would be quiet and never bring other kids home with me. Phil was always there, reeking of chewing tobacco, drooling strings of it into the chipped enamel mug he carried with him everywhere. Phil had been badly burned in a warehouse fire that left his skin blister-smooth and invested with an angry glow, as if the fire still burned somewhere inside him. The fingers of one hand were welded together.

He was right not to want me around. When we passed one another in the hallway or on the stairs, I couldn't keep my eyes from him and he saw in them no sympathy or friendliness, only disgust. He responded by touching me constantly. He knew better but could not help himself. He touched me on the shoulders, on the head, on the neck, using all the gestures of fatherly affection while measuring my horror with a cold bitter gaze, giving new pain to himself as if he had no choice.

My place was off-limits and Terry Taylor's was full of trolls, so we usually ended up at Silver's apartment. Silver was an only child, clever, skinny, malicious, a shameless coward when his big mouth brought trouble down on us. His father was a cantor who lived in Tacoma with his new wife. Silver's mother worked all day at Boeing. That meant we had the apartment to ourselves for hours at a stretch.

But first we made our rounds. As we left school we followed girls at a safe distance and offered up smart remarks. We drifted in and out of stores, palming anything that wasn't under glass. We coasted stolen tricycles down the hills around Alkai Point, standing on the seats and jumping off at the last moment to send them crashing into parked cars. Sometimes, if we had the money, we took a bus downtown and weaved through the winos around Pioneer Square to stare at guns in the windows of pawnshops. For all three of us the Luger was the weapon of choice; our passion for this pistol was profound and about the only passion we admitted to. In the presence of a Luger we stopped our continual jostling of each other and stood wide-eyed.

Television was very big on the Nazis then. Every week they screened new horrors, always with a somber narrator to remind us that this wasn't make-believe but actual history, that what we were seeing had really happened and could happen again if we did not maintain ourselves in a state of vigilance. These shows always ended the same way. Overviews of ruined Berlin. Grinning GIs rousting the defeated Aryan soldiery from their hiding places in barn and cave and sewer. Himmler dead in his cell, hollow-eyed Hess in Spandau. The now lathered-up narrator crowing, "Thus was the high-flying Prussian eagle brought to ground!" and "Thus did the little Führer and his bullyboys turn tail and run, giving up forever their dream of *The Thousand Year Reich!*"

But these glimpses of humiliation and loss lasted only a few minutes. They were tacked on as a pretense that the point of the show was to celebrate the victory of goodness over evil. We saw through this fraud, of course. We saw that the real point was to celebrate snappy uniforms and racy Mercedes staff cars and great marching, thousands of boots slamming down together on cobbled streets while banners streamed overhead and strong voices sang songs that stirred our blood though we couldn't understand a word. The point was to watch Stukas peel off and dive toward burning cities, tanks blowing holes in buildings, men with Lugers and dogs ordering people around. These shows instructed us further in the faith we were already beginning to hold: that victims are contemptible, no matter how much people pretend otherwise; that it is more fun to be inside than outside, to be arrogant than to be kind, to be with a crowd than to be alone.

Terry Silver had a Nazi armband that he swore was genuine, though anyone could see he'd made it himself. As soon as we reached his apartment Silver would get this armband from its hiding place and slip it on. Then he would strut around and treat Taylor and me like lackeys. We let him do it because of the candy Mrs. Silver left out in crystal bowls, because of the television set, and because without Silver to tell us what to do we were reduced to wandering the sidewalks, listlessly throwing rocks at signs.

First we made a few calls. Taylor and I listened in on the extension in Mrs. Silver's bedroom while Silver did the talking. He looked up people with Jewish-sounding names and screamed at them in pig German. He ordered entire banquets of Chinese food for his father and stepmother. Sometimes he called the parents of kids we didn't like and assumed the voice and manner of a Concerned Adult—teacher, coach, counselor—just touching base to ask whether there was some problem at home that might account for Paul's unusual behaviour at school the other day. Silver never laughed, never gave himself away. When he was being particularly plausible and suave, Taylor and I had to stuff Mrs. Silver's coverlet in our mouths and flail the mattress with our fists.

Then, bumping each other with our hips to make room, the three of us would press together in front of Mrs. Silver's full-length mirror to comb our hair and practice looking cool. We wore our hair long at the sides, swept back into a ducktail. The hair on top we combed toward the center and then forward, with spit curls breaking over our foreheads. My mother detested this hairdo and forbade me to wear it, which meant that I wore it everywhere but at home, sustaining the distinctness of two different styles with gobs of Butch Wax that left my hair glossy and hard and my forehead ringed with little pimples.

Unlit cigarettes dangling from the corners of our mouths, eyelids at half mast, we studied ourselves in the mirror. Spit curls. Pants pulled down low on our hips, thin white belts buckled on the side. Shirts with three-quarterlength sleeves. Collars raised behind our necks. We should have looked cool, but we didn't. Silver was emaciated. His eyes bulged, his Adam's apple protruded, his arms poked out of his sleeves like pencils with gloves stuck on the ends. Taylor had the liquid eyes and long lashes and broad blank face of a cow. I didn't look that great myself. But it wasn't really our looks that made us uncool. Coolness did not demand anything as obvious as that. Like chess or music, coolness claimed its own out of some mysterious impulse of recognition. Uncoolness did likewise. We had been claimed by uncoolness.

At five o'clock we turned on the television and watched *The Mickey Mouse Club*. It was understood that we were all holding a giant bone for Annette. This was our excuse for watching the show, and for me it was partly true. I had certain ideas of the greater world that Annette belonged to, and I wanted a place in this world. I wanted it with all the feverish, disabling hunger of first love.

At the end of every show the local station gave an address for Mousketeer Mail. I had begun writing Annette. At first I described myself in pretty much the same terms as I had in my letters to Alice, who was now very much past tense, with the difference that instead of owning a ranch my father, Cap'n Wolff, now owned a fleet of fishing boats. I was first mate, myself, and a pretty fair hand at reeling in the big ones. I gave Annette some very detailed descriptions of my contests with the friskier fellows I ran up against. I also invited her to consider the fun to be had in visiting Seattle. I told her we had lots of room. I did not tell her that I was eleven years old.

I got back some chipper official responses encouraging me to start an Annette fan club. In other words, to organize my competition. Fat chance. But when I upped the ante in my letters to her, they stopped sending me anything at all. The Disney Studio must have had a kind of secret service that monitored Mousketeer Mail for inappropriate sentiments and declarations. When my name went off the mailing list, it probably went onto some other list. But Alice had taught me about coyness. I kept writing Annette and began to imagine a terrible accident in front of her house that would almost but not quite kill me, leaving me dependent on her care and sympathy, which in time would turn to admiration, love . . .

As soon as she appeared on the show—Hi, I'm Annette!—Taylor would start moaning and Silver would lick the screen with his tongue. "Come here, baby," he'd say, "I've got six inches of piping hot flesh just for you."

We all said things like that—It was a formality—then we shut up and watched the show. Our absorption was complete. We softened. We surrendered. We joined the club. Taylor forgot himself and sucked his thumb, and Silver and I let him get away with it. We watched the Mousketeers get all excited about wholesome projects and have wimpy adventures and talk about their feelings, and we didn't laugh at them. We didn't laugh at them when they said nice things about their parents, or when they were polite to each other, or when they said, "Hey, gang . . ." We watched every minute of it, our eyes glistening in the blue light, and we went on staring at the television after they had sung the anthem and faded away into commercials for toothpaste and candy. Then, blinking and awkward, we would rouse ourselves and talk dirty about Annette.

Sometimes, when *The Mickey Mouse Club* was over, we went up to the roof. Silver's apartment building overlooked California Avenue. Though the street was busy we chose our targets carefully. Most days we didn't throw anything at all. But now and then someone would appear who had no chance of getting past us, like the man in the Thunderbird.

Thunderbirds had been out for only a year now, since '55, and because they were new and there weren't that many of them they were considered somewhat cooler than Corvettes. It was early evening. The Thunderbird was idling before a red light at the intersection, and from our perch behind the parapet we could hear the song on the radio—"Over the Mountains and across the Seas"—and hear too, just below the music, the full-throated purr of the engine. The black body glistened like obsidian. Blue smoke chugged from the twin exhausts. The top was rolled back. We could see the red leather upholstery and the blond man in the dinner jacket sitting in the driver's seat. He was young and handsome and fresh. You could almost smell the Listerine on his breath, the Mennen on his cheeks. We were looking right down at him. With the palm of his left hand he kept the beat of the song against the steering wheel. His right arm rested on the back of the empty seat beside him, which would not remain empty for long. He was on his way to pick someone up.

We held no conference. One look was enough to see that he was everything we were not, his life a progress of satisfactions we had no hope of attaining in any future we could seriously propose for ourselves.

The first egg hit the street beside him. The second egg hit the front fender. The third egg hit the trunk and splattered his shoulders and neck and hair. We looked down just long enough to tally the damage before pulling our heads back. A moment passed. Then a howl rose skyward. No words—just one solitary soul cry of disbelief. We could still hear the music coming from his radio. The light must have changed, because a horn honked, and honked again, and someone yelled something, and another voice answered harshly, and the song was suddenly lost in the noise of engines.

We rolled back and forth on the roof for a while. Just as we were getting ready to go back down to Silver's apartment, the Thunderbird screeched around the corner up the block. We could hear the driver cursing. The car moved slowly toward the light, combusting loudly. As it passed below we peered over the parapet again. The driver was scanning the sidewalks with stiff angry jerks of his head. He seemed to have no idea where the eggs had come from. We let fly again. One hit the hood with a loud boom, another landed in the seat beside him, the last exploded on the dashboard. Covered with egg and eggshell, he rose in his seat and bellowed.

There was more honking at the light. Again he tore away and again he came back, still bellowing. Six eggs were left in the carton. Each of us took two. Silver knelt by the edge, risking a few hurried glances into the street while holding his arm out behind him to keep us in check until the moment was right. Then he beckoned furiously and we reared up beside him and got rid of our eggs and dropped back out of sight before they hit. The driver was looking up at the building across the street; he never laid eyes on us. We heard the eggs smack the pavement, boom against the car. This time there was no cry of protest. The silence made me uncomfortable and in my discomfort I grinned at Silver, but Silver did not grin back. His face was purple and twitching with anger as if he had been the one set upon and outraged. He was beside himself. Breathing loudly, clenching and unclenching his jaw, he leaned over the edge and cupped his hands in front of his mouth and screamed a word I had heard only once, years before, when my father shouted it at a man who had cut him off in traffic.

"Yid!" Silver screamed, and again, "Yid!"

One day my mother and I went down to Alkai Point to watch a mock naval battle between the Odd Fellows and the Lions Club. This was during Seafair, when the hydroplane races were held. The park overlooked the harbor; we could just make out the figures on the two sailboats throwing water-balloons back and forth and trying to repel each other's boarding parties. There was a crowd in the park, and whenever one of these boarding parties got thrown back into the water everybody would laugh.

My mother was laughing with the rest. She loved to watch men goof around with each other; lifeguards, soldiers in bus stations, fraternity brothers having a car wash.

It was a clear day. Hawkers moved through the crowd, selling sun glasses and hats and Seafair souvenirs. Girls were sunning themselves on blankets. The air smelled of coconut oil.

Two men holding bottles of beer stood nearby. They kept turning and looking at us. Then one of them walked over, a pair of binoculars swinging from a strap in his hand. He was darkly tanned and wore tennis whites. He had a thin moustache and a crew cut. "Hey, Bub," he said to me, "want to give these a try?" While he adjusted the strap around my

TOBIAS WOLFF

neck and showed me how to focus the lenses, the other man came up and said something to my mother. She answered him, but continued gazing out toward the water with her hand shielding her eyes. I brought the Lions and the Odd Fellows into focus and watched them push each other overboard. They seemed so close I could see their pale bodies and the expressions of fatigue on their faces. Despite the hearty shouts they gave, they climbed the ropes with difficulty and fell back as soon as they met resistance. Each time they hit the water they stayed there a while longer, paddling just enough to keep themselves afloat, looking wearily up at the boats they were supposed to capture.

My mother accepted a beer from the man beside her. The one who'd offered me the binoculars sensed my restlessness, maybe even my jealousy. He knelt down beside me and explained the battle as if I were a little kid, but I took the binoculars off and handed them back to him.

"I don't know," my mother was saying. "We should probably get home pretty soon."

The man she'd been talking with turned to me. He was the older of the two, a tall angular man with gingercolored hair and a disjointed way of moving, as if he were always off balance. He wore Bermudas and black socks. His long face was sunburned, making his teeth look strangely prominent. "Let's ask the big fella," he said. "What say, big fella? You want to watch the fun from my place?" He pointed at a large brick house on the edge of the park.

I ignored him. "Mom," I said. "I'm hungry."

54

"He hasn't had lunch yet," my mother said.

"Lunch," the man said. "That's no problem. What do you like?" he asked me. "What's your absolute favorite thing to have for lunch?"

I looked at my mother. She was in high spirits and that made me even grimmer, because I knew they were not due to my influence. "He likes hamburgers," she told him.

"You got it," he said. He took my mother's elbow and led her across the park toward the house. I was left to follow along with the other man, who seemed to find me interesting. He wanted to know my name, where I went to school, where I lived, my mother's name, the whereabouts of my father. I was a sucker for any grown-up who asked me questions. By the time we reached the house I had forgotten to be sullen and told him everything about us.

The house was cavernous inside, hushed and cool. The windows had stained-glass medallions set within their mullioned panes. They were arched, and so were the heavy doors. The living room ceiling, ribbed with beams, curved to an arch high overhead. I sat down on the couch. The coffee table in front of me was crowded with empty beer bottles. My mother went to the open windows on the harbor side of the room. "Boy!" she said. "What a view!"

The sunburned man said, "Judd, take care of our friend."

"Come on, Bub," said the man I'd been talking to. "I'll rustle you up something to eat."

I followed him to the kitchen and sat at a counter while Judd pulled things out of the refrigerator. He slapped together a baloney sandwich and set it in front of me. He seemed to have forgotten about the hamburger. I would have said something, but I had a pretty good idea that even if I did there still wasn't going to be any hamburger.

When we came back to the living room, my mother was looking out the window through the binoculars. The sunburned man stood beside her, his head bent close to hers, one hand resting on her shoulder as he gestured with his beer bottle at some point of interest. He turned as we came in and grinned at us. "There's our guy," he said. "How's it going? You get some lunch? Judd, did you get this man some lunch?"

"Yes sir."

"Great! That's the ticket! Have a seat, Rosemary. Right over here. Sit down, Jack, that's the boy. You like peanuts? Great! Judd, bring him some peanuts. And for Christ's sake get these bottles out of here." He sat next to my mother on the couch and smiled steadily at me while Judd stuck his fingers into the bottles and carried them clinking away. Judd returned with a dish of nuts and left with the rest of the bottles.

"There you go, Jack. Dig in! Dig in!" He watched me eat a few handfuls, nodding to himself as if I were acting in accordance with some prediction he had made. "You're an athlete," he said. "It's written all over you. The eyes, the build. What do you play, Jack, what's your game?"

"Baseball," I said. This was somewhere in the neighborhood of truth. In Florida I'd played nearly every day, and gotten good at it. But I hadn't played much since. I wasn't an athlete and I didn't look like one, but I was glad he thought so.

"Baseball!" he cried. "Judd, what did I tell you?"

Judd had taken a chair on the other side of the room, apart from the rest of us. He raised his eyebrows and shook his head at the other man's perspicacity.

My mother laughed and said something teasing. She called the man Gil.

"Wait a minute!" he said. "You think I'm just shooting the bull? Judd, what did I say about Jack here? What did I say he played?"

Judd crossed his dark legs. "Baseball," he said.

"All right," Gil said. "All right, I hope we've got *that* straightened out. Jack. Back to you. What other activities do you enjoy?"

"I like to ride bikes," I said, "but I don't have one."

I saw the good humor leave my mother's face, just as I knew it would. She looked at me coldly and I looked coldly back at her. The subject of bicycles turned us into enemies. Our problem was that I wanted a bike and she didn't have enough money to buy me one. She had no money at all. She had explained this to me many times. I understood perfectly, but not having a bike seemed too hard a thing to bear in silence.

Gil mugged disbelief. He looked from me to my mother and back to me. "No bike? A boy with no bike?"

"We'll discuss this later," my mother told me.

"I just said—"

57

"I know what you said." She frowned and looked away.

"Hold on!" Gil said. "Just hold on. Now what's the story here, Mom? Are you seriously telling me that this boy does not have a bicycle?"

My mother said, "He's going to have to wait a little longer, that's all."

"Boys can't wait for bikes, Rosemary. Boys need bikes now!"

My mother shrugged and smiled tightly, as she usually did when she was cornered. "I don't have the money," she said quietly.

The word *money* left a heavy silence in its wake.

Then Gil said, "Judd, let's have another round. See if there's some ginger ale for the slugger."

Judd rose and left the room.

Gil said, "What kind of bicycle would you like to have, Jack?"

"A Schwinn, I guess."

"Really? You'd rather have a Schwinn than an English racer?" He saw me hesitate. "Or would you rather have an English racer?"

I nodded.

"Well then, say so! I can't read your mind."

"I'd rather have an English racer."

"That's the way. Now what *kind* of English racer are we talking about?"

Judd brought the drinks. Mine was bitter. I recognized it as Collins mix.

My mother leaned forward and said, "Gil."

He held up his hand. "What kind, Jack?"

"Raleigh," I told him. Gil smiled and I smiled back.

"Champagne taste," he said. "Go for the best, that's the way. What color?"

"Red."

"Red. Fair enough. I think we can manage that. Did you get all that, Judd? One bicycle, English racer, Raleigh, red."

"Got it," Judd said.

My mother said thanks but she couldn't accept it. Gil said it was for me to accept, not her. She began to argue, not halfheartedly but with resolve. Gil wouldn't hear a word of it. At one point he even put his hands over his ears.

At last she gave up. She leaned back and drank from her beer. And I saw that in spite of what she'd said she was really happy at the way things had turned out, not only because it meant the end of these arguments of ours but also because, after all, she wanted very much for me to have a bicycle.

"How are the peanuts, Jack?" Gil asked.

I said they were fine.

"Great," he said. "That's just great."

GIL AND MY mother had a few more beers and talked while Judd and I watched the hydroplane qualifying heats on television. In the early evening Judd drove us back to the boardinghouse. My mother and I lay on our beds for a while with the lights off, feeling the breeze, listening to the treetops rustle outside.

She asked if I would mind staying home alone that night. She had been invited out for dinner. "Who with?" I asked. "Gil and Judd?"

"Gil," she said.

"No," I said. I was glad. This would firm things up.

The room filled with shadows. My mother got up and took a bath, then put on a full blue skirt and an off-the-shoulder Mexican blouse and the fine turquoise jewelry my father had bought her when they were driving through Arizona before the war. Earrings, necklace, heavy bracelet, concha belt. She'd picked up some sun that day; the blue of the turquoise seemed especially vivid, and so did the blue of her eyes. She dabbed perfume behind her ears, in the crook of her elbow, on her wrists. She rubbed her wrists together and touched them to her neck and chest. She turned from side to side, checking herself in the mirror. Then she stopped turning and studied herself head-on in a sober way. Without taking her eyes from the mirror she asked me how she looked. Really pretty, I told her.

"That's what you always say."

"Well, it's true."

"Good," she said. She gave herself one last look and we went downstairs.

Marian and Kathy came in while my mother was cooking dinner for me. They had her turn around for them, both of them smiling and exclaiming, and Marian pushed her away from the stove and finished making my dinner so she wouldn't get stains on her blouse. My mother was cagey with their questions. They teased her about this mystery man, and when the horn honked outside they followed her down the hall, adjusting her clothes, patting her hair, issuing final instructions.

"He should have come to the door," Marian said when they were back in the kitchen.

Kathy shrugged, and looked down at the table. She was hugely pregnant by this time and may have felt unsure of her right to decide the finer points of dating.

"He should have come to the door," Marian said again.

I SLEPT BADLY that night. I always did when my mother went out, which wasn't often these days. She came back late. I listened to her walk up the stairs and down the hall to our room. The door opened and closed. She stood just inside for a moment, then crossed the room and sat down on her bed. She was crying softly. "Mom?" I said. When she didn't answer I got up and went over to her. "What's wrong, Mom?" She looked at me, tried to say something, shook her head. I sat beside her and put my arms around her. She was gasping as if someone had held her underwater.

I rocked her and murmured to her. I was practiced at this and happy doing it, not because she was unhappy but because she needed me, and to be needed made me feel capable. Soothing her soothed me.

She exhausted herself, and I helped her into bed. She became giddy then, laughing and making fun of herself, but she didn't let go of my hand until she fell asleep.

In the morning we were shy with each other. I somehow managed not to ask her my question. That night I continued to master myself, but my self-mastery seemed like an act; I knew I was too weak to keep it up.

My mother was reading.

"Mom?" I said.

She looked up.

"What about the Raleigh?"

She went back to her book without answering. I did not ask again.

M arian and Kathy and my mother decided to rent a house together. My mother offered to find the house, and so she did. It was the most scabrous eyesore in West Seattle. Paint hung in strips off the sides, the bare wood weathered to a gray, antlerish sheen. The yard was kneehigh in weeds. The sagging eaves had been propped up with long planks, and the front steps were rotted through. To get inside you had to go around to the back door. Behind the house was a partly collapsed barn that little kids liked to sneak into, drawn there by the chance to play with broken glass and rusty tools.

My mother took it on the spot. The price was right, next to nothing, and she believed in its possibilities, a word used often by the man who showed it to her. He insisted on meeting us there at night and led us through the house like a thief, describing its good points in a whisper. My mother, listening with narrowed eyes to show that she was shrewd and would not be easily taken in, ended up agreeing with him that the place was just a few steps away from being a real nice home. She signed the contract on the hood of the man's car while he held a flashlight over the paper.

The other houses on the street were small, obsessively groomed Cape Cods and colonials with lawns like putting greens. Ivy grew on the chimneys. Each of the colonials had a black, spread-winged eagle above its door. The people who lived in these houses came outside to watch us move in. They looked very glum. Later on we found out that our house, the original farmhouse in the area, had recently been scheduled for demolition and then spared at the last hour by the cynical manipulations of its owner.

Kathy and Marian went mute when they saw it. Shoulders hunched, faces set, they carried their boxes up the walk without looking to right or left. That night they slammed and banged and muttered in their rooms. But in the end my mother wore them down. She gave no sign that she saw any difference between our house and the houses of our neighbors except for a few details that we ourselves, during a spare hour now and then, could easily put right. She helped us picture the house after we had made these repairs. She was so good at making us see it her way that we began to feel as if everything needful had already been done, and settled in without lifting a finger to save the house from its final decrepitude.

Soon after we took the house, Kathy had a baby boy, Willy. Willy was a clown. Even when he was alone he cackled and squawked like a parrot. The sweet, almost cloying smell of milk filled the house.

Kathy and my mother worked at their jobs downtown while Marian kept the house and did the meals and looked after Willy. She was supposed to take care of me, too, but I ran around with Taylor and Silver after school and didn't come home until just before I knew my mother would arrive.

When Marian asked me where I'd been I told her lies. She knew I was lying, but she couldn't control me or even convince my mother that I needed controlling. My mother had faith in me. She didn't have faith in discipline. Her father, Daddy, had given her plenty and she had yet to see the profit from it.

Daddy was a great believer in the rod. When my mother was still in her cradle he slapped her for sucking her thumb. To correct her toddler's habit of walking with her toes turned slightly inward he forced her to walk with her toes turned out, like a duck. Once she started school, Daddy spanked her almost every night on the theory that she must have done something wrong that day whether he knew about it or not. He told her that he was going to spank her well in advance, as the family sat down to dinner, so she could think about it while she ate and listened to him talk about the stock market and the fool in the White House. After dessert he spanked her. Then she had to kiss him and say, "Thank you, Daddy, for earning the delicious meal."

My grandmother was a gentle woman. She tried to defend her daughter, but her heart was bad and she couldn't even defend herself. Whenever she was bedridden, Daddy would read to her from the works of Mary Baker Eddy to prove that her suffering was illusory, the result of improper thinking. On their Sunday drives he boosted her pulse by going through stop signs and racing trains to railroad crossings. Once he scooped a man onto his hood and carried him at speed for several blocks, screaming, "Get off my car!"

My mother was on her own with Daddy. When she started high school he forced her to wear bloomers—pink silk bloomers with ruffled legs. He'd brought several pairs home with him from a cruise to China, where they were still in vogue among missionaries' wives. He badgered her into smoking cigarettes so she wouldn't eat much, and when they went to restaurants he made her fill up on bread. She wasn't allowed to go out with boys. But the boys wouldn't give up. One night some of them parked in front of her house and sang "When It's Springtime in the Rockies." When they called out, "Goodnight, Rosemary!" Daddy went berserk. He ran into the street waving his Navy .45. As the driver sped off Daddy fired several shots at a boy in the rumble seat, who ducked just before two bullets whanged into the metal over his head. My grandmother collapsed and had to be given digitalis.

Daddy didn't let it go at that. In full uniform he prowled the school parking lot the next morning, inspecting cars for bullet holes.

My mother took off a few months after her mother died, when she was still a girl. But Daddy left some marks on her. One of them was a strange docility, almost paralysis, with men of the tyrant breed. Another was a contradictory hatred of coercion. She'd never been able to spank me. The few times she tried I came away laughing. She couldn't even raise her voice convincingly. That wasn't the way she wanted to be with me, and she didn't think I needed it anyway.

Marian thought otherwise. Sometimes at night I heard the two of them arguing about me, Marian strident, my mother quiet and implacable. It was just the age I was going through, she said. I'd grow out of it. I was a good boy.

ON HALLOWEEN, TAYLOR and Silver and I broke out some windows in the school cafeteria. The next day two policemen came to school and several boys with bad reputations were called out of class to talk to them. Nobody thought of us, not even of Taylor, who had a recorded history of window breaking. The reason nobody thought of us was that at school, in the presence of really tough kids who got into fights and talked back to teachers, we were colorless and mild.

At the end of the day the principal came on the public address system and announced that the guilty parties had been identified. Before taking action, however, he wanted to give these individuals a chance to come forward on their own. A voluntary confession now would work greatly in their favor later on. Taylor and Silver and I avoided looking at each other. We knew it was a bluff, because we'd been in the same classroom all day long. Otherwise the trick would have worked. We didn't trust each other, and any suspicion that one of us was weakening would have created a stampede of betrayal.

We got away with it. A week later we came back after a movie to break some more windows, then chickened out when a car turned into the parking lot and sat there with its engine running for a few minutes before driving away.

Instead of making us more careful, the interest of the police in what we'd done elated us. We became self-important, cocksure, insane in our arrogance. We broke windows. We broke streetlights. We opened the doors of cars parked on hills and released the emergency brakes so they smashed into the cars below. We set bags of shit on fire and left them on doorsteps, but people didn't stamp them out as they were supposed to do; instead they waited with weary expressions as the bags burned, now and then looking up to scan the shadows from which they felt us watching them.

We did these things in darkness and in the light of day, moving always to the sound of breaking glass and yowling cats and grinding metal.

And we stole. At first we stole as part of our general hoodlum routine, and for Taylor and Silver it never had any more importance than that. But for me the stealing was serious business, so much so that I dissembled its seriousness, not letting Taylor and Silver see the hold it had on me. I was a thief. By my own estimation, a master thief. When I cruised the aisles of dime stores, lingering over jackknives and model cars, a bland expression on my face, looking more innocent than an innocent person has any business looking, I imagined that the saleswomen who sometimes glanced over at me saw an earnest young shopper instead of a transparent little klepto. And when I finally managed to steal something I figured I was getting away with it because I was so sharp, and not because these women had been on their feet all day and were too tired to deal with a shoplifter and the trouble he would cause them: his false outrage, then his terror, his weeping, the triumphant descent of the manager, policemen, paperwork, the hollowness they would feel when it was over.

I hid the things I stole. Now and then I took them out and turned them over in my hands, dully considering them. Out of the store they did not interest me, except for the jack-knives, which I threw at trees until the blades broke off.

A FEW MONTHS after we moved into the house Marian got engaged to her marine boyfriend. Then Kathy got engaged to a man in her office. Marian thought my mother should get engaged too, and tried to fix her up. She set in motion a brief parade of suitors. One by one they came up the walk, stared at the broken steps, went around to the back; then, entering the kitchen, braced themselves and put on joviality like a party hat. Even I could see the hopelessness in their imitation of gaiety though not its source in their belief, already sufficiently formed to make itself come true, that this woman too would find them unacceptable.

There was a marine who did tricks for me with lengths of string tied to his fingers, and seemed unwilling to leave the house with my mother. There was a man who arrived drunk and had to be sent away in a cab. There was an old man who, my mother told me later, tried to borrow money from her. And then came Dwight.

Dwight was a short man with curly brown hair and sad, restless brown eyes. He smelled of gasoline. His legs were small for his thick-chested body, but what they lacked in length they made up for in spring; he had an abrupt, surprising way of springing to his feet. He dressed like no one I'd ever met before—two-tone shoes, hand-painted tie, monogrammed blazer with a monogrammed handkerchief in the breast pocket. Dwight kept coming back, which made him chief among the suitors. My mother said he was a good dancer—he could really make those shoes of his get up and go. Also he was very nice, very considerate.

I didn't worry about him. He was too short. He was a mechanic. His clothes were wrong. I didn't know why they were wrong, but they were. We hadn't come all the way out here to end up with him. He didn't even live in Seattle; he lived in a place called Chinook, a tiny village three hours north of Seattle, up in the Cascade Mountains. Besides, he'd already been married. He had three kids of his own living with him, all teenagers. I knew my mother would never let herself get tangled up in a mess like that.

And even though Dwight kept driving down from the mountains to see my mother, every other weekend at first, then every weekend, he seemed to sense the futility of his case. His attentions to my mother were puppyish, fawning, as if he knew that the odds of getting his hands on her were pathetically slim and that even being in her presence was a piece of luck that depended on his displaying at every moment deference, bounce, optimism, and all manner of good cheer.

He tried too hard. No eye is quicker to detect that kind of effort than the eye of a competitor who also happens to be a child. I seized on and stored away every nuance of Dwight's abjection, his habit of licking his lips, the way his eyes darted from face to face to search out warning signs of disagreement or boredom, his uncertain smile, the phony timbre of his laughter at jokes he didn't really get. Nobody could just go to the kitchen and make a drink, Dwight had to jump up and do it himself. Nobody could open a door or put on a coat without his help. They couldn't even smoke their own cigarettes, they had to take one of Dwight's and submit to a prolonged drama of ignition: the unsheathing of his monogrammed Zippo from its velvet case; the snapping open of the top against his pant leg; the presentation of the tall flame with its crown of oily smoke—then the whole ritual in reverse.

I was a good mimic, or at least a cruel one, and Dwight was an easy target. I went to work as soon as he left the house. My mother and Kathy tried not to laugh but they did, and so did Marian, though she never really abandoned herself to it. "Dwight's not that bad," she would say to my mother, and my mother would nod. "He's very nice," Marian would add, and my mother would nod again and say, "Jack, that's enough."

We spent Thanksgiving in Chinook with Dwight and his kids. Snow had fallen a few nights earlier. It had melted in the valley but still covered the trees on the upper slopes, which were purple with shadow when we arrived. Though it was still late afternoon the sun had already set behind the mountains.

Dwight's kids came out to meet us when we drove up. The two oldest, a boy and a girl, waited at the bottom of the steps as a girl about my age ran up to my mother and threw her arms around her waist. I was completely disgusted. The girl was pinch-faced and scrawny, and on the back of her head she had a bald spot the size of a silver dollar. She made a kind of crooning noise as she clutched my mother, who, instead of pushing this person away, laughed and hugged her back.

"This is Pearl," Dwight said, and somehow freed my mother from her grasp. Pearl looked over at me. She did not smile, and neither did I.

We walked up to the house and met the other two. Both of them were taller than Dwight. Skipper had a wedge-shaped head, flat in the back and sharp in front, with close-set eyes and a long blade of a nose. He wore a crew cut. Skipper regarded me with polite lack of interest and turned his attention to my mother, greeting her with grave but perfect courtesy. Norma just said "Hi!" and ruffled my hair. I looked up at her, and until we left Chinook two days later I stopped looking at her only when I was asleep or when someone walked between us.

Norma was seventeen, ripe and lovely. Her lips were full and red, always a little swollen-looking as if she'd just woken up, and she moved sleepily too, languidly, stretching often. When she stretched, her blouse went taut and parted slightly between the buttons, showing milky slices of belly. She had the whitest skin. Thick red hair that she pushed sleepily back from her forehead. Green eyes flecked with brown. She used lavender water, and the faint sweetness of the smell got mixed up with the warmth she gave off. Sometimes, just fooling around, thinking nothing of it, she would put her arm around my shoulder and bump me with her hip, or pull me up against her.

If Norma noticed my unblinking stare she took it for granted. She never seemed surprised by it, or embarrassed. When our eyes met she smiled.

We brought our bags inside and took a tour of the house. It wasn't really a house, but half of a barracks where German prisoners of war had been quartered. After the war the barracks had been converted to a duplex. A family named Miller lived on one side, Dwight's family on the other, in three bedrooms that faced the kitchen, dining room, and living room across a narrow hallway. The rooms were small and dark. Her arms crossed over her chest, my mother peered into them and gushed falsely. Dwight sensed her reserve. He waved his hands around, declaring the plans he had for renovation. My mother couldn't help but offer a few suggestions of her own, which Dwight admired so much that he adopted them all, right then and there.

AFTER DINNER MY mother went out with Dwight to meet some of his friends. I helped Norma and Pearl do the dishes, then Skipper took out the Monopoly board and we played a couple of games. Pearl won both of them because she cared so much. She watched us suspiciously and recited rules at us while she gloated over her rising pile of deeds and money. After she won she told the rest of us everything we'd done wrong.

My mother woke me when she came in. We were sharing the sofa bed in the living room, and she kept turning and plumping the pillow. She couldn't settle down. When I asked what was wrong she said, "Nothing. Go to sleep." Then she raised herself up on one elbow and whispered, "What do you think?"

"They're okay," I said. "Norma's nice."

"They're all nice," she said. She lay back again. Still whispering, she told me she liked them all, but felt a little hurried. She didn't want to hurry into anything.

That made sense, I said.

She said she was doing really well at work. She felt like she was finally starting to get somewhere. She didn't want to stop, not right now. Did I know what she meant?

I said I knew exactly what she meant.

Is that selfish? she asked. Marian thought she should get married. Marian thought I needed a father in the worst way. But she didn't *want* to get married, not really. Not now, anyway. Maybe later, when she felt ready, but not now.

That was fine with me, I said. Later would be fine.

THE NEXT DAY was Thanksgiving. After breakfast Dwight packed everyone into the car and drove us around Chinook. Chinook was a company village owned by Seattle City Light. A couple of hundred people lived there in neat rows of houses and converted barracks, all white with green trim. The lanes between the houses had been hedged with rhododendron, and Dwight said the flowers bloomed all summer long. The village had the gracious, well-tended look of an old military camp, and that was what everyone called it—the camp. Most of the men worked at the powerhouse or at one of three dams along the Skagit. The river ran through the village, a deep, powerful river crowded on both sides by steep mountains. These mountains faced each other across a valley half a mile wide at the point where Chinook had been built. The slopes were heavily forested, the trees taking root even in granite outcroppings and gullies of scree. Mists hung in the treetops.

Dwight took his time showing us around. After we had seen the village, he drove us upstream along a narrow road dropping sheer to the river on one side and overhung by boulders on the other. As he drove he listed the advantages of life in Chinook. The air. The water. No crime, no juvenile delinquency. For scenery all you had to do was step out your front door, which you never had to lock. Hunting. Fishing. In fact the Skagit was one of the best trout streams in the world. Ted Williams—who, not many people realized, was a world-class angler as well as a baseball great, not to mention a war hero—had been fishing here for years.

Pearl sat up front between Dwight and my mother. She had her head on my mother's shoulder and was almost in her lap. I sat in the backseat between Skipper and Norma. They were quiet. At one point my mother turned and asked, "How about you guys? How do you like it here?"

They looked at each other. Skipper said, "Fine."

"Fine," Norma said. "It's just a little isolated, is all."

"Not that isolated," Dwight said.

"Well," Norma said, "maybe not *that* isolated. Pretty isolated, though."

"There's plenty to do here if you kids would just take a little initiative," Dwight said. "When I was growing up we didn't have all the things you kids have, we didn't have record players, we didn't have TVs, all of that, but we were never bored. We were never bored. We used our imaginations. We read the classics. We played musical instruments. There is absolutely no excuse for a kid to be bored, not in my book there isn't. You show me a bored kid and I'll show you a lazy kid."

My mother glanced at Dwight, then turned back to Norma and Skipper. "You'll be graduating this year, right?" she said to Skipper.

He nodded.

"And you have another year," she said to Norma.

"One more year," Norma said. "One more year and watch my dust."

"How's the school here?"

"They don't have one. Just a grade school. We go to Concrete."

"Concrete?"

"Concrete High," Norma said.

"That's the name of a *town*?"

"We passed it on the way up," Dwight said. "Concrete."

"Concrete," my mother repeated.

"It's a few miles downriver," Dwight said.

"Forty miles," Norma said.

"Come off it," Dwight said. "It's not that far."

"Thirty-nine miles," Skipper said. "Exactly. I measured it on the odometer."

"What's the difference!" Dwight said. "You'd bellyache just as much if the goddamned school was next door. If all you can do is complain, I would thank you to just stow it. Just kindly stow it." Dwight kept looking back as he talked. His lower lip was curled out, and his bottom teeth showed. The car wandered the road.

"I'm in fifth grade," Pearl said.

Nobody answered her.

We drove on for a while. Then my mother asked Dwight to pull over. She wanted to take some pictures. She had Dwight and Norma and Skipper and Pearl stand together on the side of the road with snowy peaks sticking up behind them. Then Norma grabbed the camera and started ordering everyone around. The last picture she took was of me and Pearl. "Closer!" she yelled. "Come on! Okay, now hold hands. Hold hands! You know, *hands*? Like on the end of your arms?" She ran up to us, took Pearl's left hand, put it in my right hand, wrapped my fingers around it, then ran back to her vantage point and aimed the camera at us.

Pearl let her hand go dead limp. So did I. We both stared at Norma. "Jeez," she said. "Dead on arrival."

On the way back to Chinook my mother said, "Dwight, I didn't know you played an instrument. What do you play?"

Dwight was chewing on an unlit cigar. He took it out of his mouth. "A little piano," he said. "Mainly sax. Alto sax."

Skipper and Norma looked quickly at each other, then looked away again, out the windows.

WHEN DWIGHT FIRST invited us to Chinook he'd won me over by mentioning that the rifle club was going to hold a turkey shoot. If I wanted to, he said, I could bring my Winchester along and enter the contest. I hadn't fired or even held my rifle since we left Salt Lake. Every couple of weeks or so I tore the house apart looking for it, but my mother had it hidden somewhere else, probably in her office downtown.

I thought of the trip to Chinook as a reunion with my rifle. During art period I made drawings of it and showed them to Taylor and Silver, who affected disbelief in its existence. I also painted a picture that depicted me sighting down the the barrel of my rifle at a big gobbler with rolling eyes and long red wattles.

The turkey shoot was at noon. Dwight and Pearl and my mother and I drove down to the firing range while Skipper went off to work on a car that he was customizing and Norma stayed home to cook. Not until we reached the range did Dwight get around to telling me that in fact there would be no turkey at this turkey shoot. The targets were paper— regulation match targets. They weren't even giving a turkey away; the prize was a smoked Virginia ham. *Turkey shoot* was just a figure of speech, Dwight said. He thought everybody knew that.

He also let drop, casually, as if the information were of no consequence, that I would not be allowed to shoot after all. It was for grown-ups, not kids. That was all they needed, a bunch of kids running around with guns.

"But you said I could."

Dwight was assembling my Winchester, which he apparently meant to use himself. "They just told me a couple of days ago," he said.

I could tell he was lying—that he'd known all along. I couldn't do a thing but stand there and look at him. Pearl, smiling a little, watched me.

"Dwight," my mother said, "you did tell him."

He said, "I don't make the rules, Rosemary."

I started to argue, but my mother gave my shoulder a hard squeeze. When I glanced up at her she shook her head.

Dwight couldn't figure out how the rifle fit together, so I did it for him while he looked on. "That," he said, "is the most stupidly constructed firearm I have ever seen, bar none."

A man with a clipboard came up to us. He was collecting entry fees. After Dwight paid him he started to move off, but my mother stopped him and held out some money. He looked at it, then down at his clipboard.

"Wolff," she said. "Rosemary Wolff."

Still studying his clipboard, he asked if she wanted to shoot.

She said she did.

He looked over at Dwight, who busied himself with the rifle. Then he dropped his eyes again and mumbled something about the rules.

"This is an NRA club, isn't it?" my mother asked.

He nodded.

"Well, I am a dues-paying member of the NRA, and that gives me the right to participate in the activities of other chapters when I'm away from my own." She said all of this very pleasantly.

Finally he took the money. "You'll be the only woman shooting," he said.

She smiled.

He wrote her name down. "Why not?" he said suddenly, uncertainly. "Why the heck not." He gave her a number and wandered off to another group of shooters.

Dwight's number was called early. He fired his ten rounds in rapid succession, hardly pausing for breath, and got a rotten score. A couple of his shots hadn't even hit the paper. When his score was announced he handed my mother the rifle. "Where'd you get this blunderbuss, anyway?" he asked me.

My mother answered. "A friend of mine gave it to him."

"Some friend," he said. "That thing is a menace. You ought to get rid of it. It shoots wild." He added, "The bore is probably rusted out."

"The bore is perfect," I said.

My mother's number should have been called after Dwight's, but it wasn't. One man after another went up to the line while she stood there watching. I got antsy and cold. After a long wait I walked over to the river and tried to skip rocks. A mist drifted over the water. My fingers grew numb but I kept at it until the sound of rifle fire stopped, leaving a silence in which I felt too much alone. When I came back my mother had finished her turn. She was standing around with some of the men. Others were putting their rifles in their cars, passing bottles back and forth, calling to each other as they drove away into the dusk.

"You missed me!" she said when I came up.

I asked her how she had done.

"Dwight brought in a ringer," one of the men said.

"Did you win?"

She nodded.

"You won? No kidding?"

She struck a pose with the rifle.

I waited while my mother joked around with the men, laughing, trading mild insults, flushed with cold and the pleasure of being admired. Then she said good-bye and we walked toward the car. I said, "I didn't know you were a member of the NRA."

"I'm a little behind in my dues," she said.

Dwight and Pearl were sitting in the front seat with the ham between them. Neither of them spoke when we got in. Dwight pulled away fast and drove straight back to the house, where he clomped down the hall to his room and closed the door behind him.

We joined Norma and Skipper in the kitchen. Norma had taken the turkey out of the oven, and the house was rich with its smell. When she found out that my mother had won, she said, "Oh boy, now we're really in for it. He thinks he's some kind of big hunter."

"He killed a deer once," Pearl said.

"That was with the car," Norma said.

Skipper got up and went down the hall to Dwight's room. A few minutes later they both came back, Dwight stiff and awkward. Skipper teased him in a shy, affectionate way, and Dwight took it well, and my mother acted as if nothing had happened. Then Dwight perked up and made drinks for the two of them and pretty soon we were having a good time. We sat down at the beautiful table Norma had laid for us, and we ate turkey and dressing and candied yams and giblet gravy and cranberry sauce. After we ate, we sang. We sang "Harvest Moon," "Side by Side," "Moonlight Bay," "Birmingham Jail," and "High above Cayuga's Waters." I got compliments for knowing all the words. We toasted

Norma for cooking the turkey, and my mother for winning the turkey shoot.

My mother was still flushed, expansive. All the talk about turkey reminded her of a Thanksgiving she and my brother and I had spent on a turkey farm in Connecticut after the war. Housing was scarce, and we were broke, so my father had boarded us with these turkey farmers while he went down to work in Peru. The turkey farmers were novices. Before Thanksgiving they'd butchered their birds in an unheated shed, and all the blood froze in their bodies and turned them purple. The local butcher came out for a look. He suggested that the birds be kept in a warm bath for a few days—maybe that would loosen things up and turn them pink. The bath they used was ours. For almost two weeks we had these bumpy blue carcasses floating in the tub.

Dwight was quiet after my mother told her story. Then he told one of his own about a Thanksgiving he'd spent in the Philippines, when starving Japanese soldiers ran out of the jungle and grabbed food right off the chow line, and nobody even tried to shoot them.

That story reminded Pearl of Chinese checkers. Dwight and Skipper refused to play, but the rest of us joined in. First we played as free agents and then in teams. Pearl and I played the last round together. It was close—very close. When Pearl made the winning move we jumped up and down, and crowed, and pounded each other on the back.

*   *   *

DWIGHT DROVE US down to Seattle early the next morning. He stopped on the bridge leading out of camp so we could see the salmon in the water below. He pointed them out to us, dark shapes among the rocks. They had come all the way from the ocean to spawn here, Dwight said, and then they would die. They were already dying. The change from salt to fresh water had turned their flesh rotten. Long strips of it hung off their bodies, waving in the current.

Taylor and Silver and I sometimes hung out in the bathroom during lunch hour. We smoked cigarettes and combed our hair and exchanged interesting facts not available to the general public about women.

It was just after Thanksgiving. I told Taylor and Silver and a couple of weed fiends who practically lived in the bathroom the story of how I'd killed the turkey in Chinook. "I mean I blew it *off*, man—I blew his fucking head right *off!*"

At first nobody responded. Silver did the French inhale, then slowly blew the smoke toward the ceiling. "With a .22," he said.

"Fuckin' A," I said. "Winchester .22. Pump."

"Wolff," he said, "you are so full of shit."

"Fuck you, Silver. I don't care what you think."

"All a .22 would do is just make a hole in his head."

I took a drag and let the smoke come out of my mouth as I talked. "One bullet, maybe."

"Oh. Oh, I see—you hit him more than once. While he was flying. In the head."

I nodded.

Silver howled. The other guys were also manifesting signs of disbelief. "Fuck you, Silver," I said, and when he howled again I said, "Fuck. You. Fuck. You." Still saying this, I went over to the wall, which had just been repainted, and took out my comb. It was a girl's comb. We all carried them, tails sticking out of our back pockets. With the tail of the comb I scratched FUCK YOU into the soft paint and once more told Silver, "Fuck you."

The two weed fiends ditched their cigarettes and cleared out. So did Silver and Taylor. I threw away the comb and followed.

During the first period after lunch the vice-principal visited each classroom and demanded the names of those responsible for the obscenity that had been written in the boys' lavatory. He said that he was fed up with the delinquent behavior of a few rotten apples. They had names. Well, he wanted those names, and he was going to get them if he had to keep every single one of us here all night long.

The vice-principal was new and hard-nosed; he meant what he said. I knew he wouldn't let this drop, that he would keep at it until he caught me. I got scared. Even more than his anger, his righteousness scared me to the point where my stomach cramped up. As the afternoon went on the cramp got worse and I had to go to the nurse's office. That was where the vice-principal finally came for me.

He kicked at the cot where I lay doubled up and sweating. "Get up," he said. I gave him a confused look and said, "What?"

"Get moving. Now!"

I sat up partway, still miming incomprehension. The school nurse came to the doorway and asked what the problem was. The vice-principal told her I was faking.

"I'm not either," I said hotly.

"He's definitely in pain," she told him.

"He's faking it," the vice-principal said, and explained that this was nothing but a stratagem to avoid punishment for something disgusting I had done. The nurse turned to me with a quizzical expression. She had been warm and gentle; I couldn't bear for her to think that I was the kind of person who took advantage of other people's kindness, or wrote filth on bathroom walls. And at that moment I wasn't.

I began to say something along this line, but the vice-principal wasn't having any. "Let's go," he said. He grabbed one of my ears and brought me to my feet. "I'm not here to bandy words with you."

The nurse stared at him. "Now wait just a minute," she said.

He pulled me into the corridor and down toward his office, jerking on my ear so that I had to walk sideways and keep my face toward the ceiling, stumbling all the way and spastically waving my arms.

"I'm going to call his mother," the nurse said. "Right now!"

"I already did," the vice-principal said.

BY THE TIME my mother arrived, I'd spent almost an hour with the vice-principal and had become completely convinced of my own innocence. The more I insisted on it the angrier he got, and the angrier he got the more impossible it was for me to believe that I had done anything to deserve such anger. He was, I knew, very close to hitting me; this made me feel a contempt for him that he could see, which in turn brought him closer to violence, inflating even further my sense of injury and innocence. And as his rage grew so did my contempt, because I saw that it was not self-restraint that kept him from hitting me but some kind of institutional restraint.

But he still had me scared. It was like being lunged at by a dog on the end of its leash.

Things stood thus when my mother came in. She'd spoken with the school nurse and immediately asked the vice-principal what he thought he was doing, hauling me around by the ears. He said that was beside the point, Mrs. Wolff, let's not muddy the water here, but she said, No, to her it wasn't beside the point at all. She faced him across his desk. She was erect, pale, and unfriendly.

The point, he told her, was that I had violated school property and the law. Not to mention decency.

My mother looked over at me. I saw how tired she was, and she must have seen the pain I was in. I shook my head.

"You're mistaken," she told him.

He laughed disagreeably. Then he set out his case, which consisted of eyewitness testimony by two boys who had been in the lavatory at the time the obscene words in question were inscribed on the wall.

"What obscene words?" she asked.

He hesitated. Then, demurely, he said, "Fuck you."

"That's one obscene word," my mother said.

He pondered this. He said that, given the particular context, he considered *you* to be an obscene word as well.

I said I didn't do it.

"If he says he didn't do it, he didn't do it," my mother said. "He doesn't lie."

"Well, I don't either!" The vice-principal rocked forward onto his feet. He opened the door and beckoned to the weed fiends, who were waiting in the outer office. They came in together and after a hangdog glance in my direction serially mumbled their dismal narrative at the floor, while I looked at them with brazen incredulity.

When they were done the vice-principal gave them passes and sent them out. He was acting very much in control now, very much on top of the situation.

"They're lying," I said.

His placidity fell off like a mask. *"Why?"* he asked. "Give me one reason."

"I don't know," I said, "but they are."

"We're not getting anywhere," my mother said. "I think I'd better talk to the principal."

The vice-principal said that he had been given full authority in this case. He was in charge. We'd better realize that what he said went.

But my mother would not be moved. And in the end we got in to see the principal.

The principal was a furtive, whey-faced man who feared children and avoided us by staying in his office all day. He was right to avoid us. He wore his weakness in a way that excited belligerence and cruelty. When my mother and I came into his office, he insisted on making small talk with her as if she had just dropped by to see how things were going.

At one point he leaned over and peered at my fingers. "Is that nicotine?" he asked.

"No sir."

"I hope not." He leaned back. His jacket parted, revealing green suspenders. "Let me tell you a story," he said. "Take it for what it's worth. I'm not accusing you of anything, but if you hear something you can use, so much the better." He smiled and made a steeple of his fingers. "I used to smoke cigarettes. I started smoking in college because of peer pressure, and before I knew it I was up to a couple of packs a day. Those were real cigarettes, too, not with the filters like you have now. The first thing I would do when I woke up in the morning was reach for a cigarette, and I always had a cigarette before I went to bed at night.

"Well, one night I went to have my cigarette and lo and behold, the pack was empty. I had run completely out. It was late, too late to wake up anyone else in the dorm. Normally I would have just taken a couple of butts out of the ashtray, but it so happened that when I finished studying I had emptied the ashtray into my wastebasket and dumped it down the incinerator shaft. So there I was, without my nightly cigarette."

He paused, contemplating his outrageous youthful self. "You know what I did? I'll tell you. I started walking in circles with my heart beating a mile a minute. 'What'll I do? What'll I do?' I kept asking myself. What I ended up doing was, I ended up running downstairs to the lounge. The ashtrays were empty. Then I started going through the garbage cans in the hallway. At last I found one with butts in it. But as I reached down—right down into a *garbage* can—I suddenly thought, 'Whoa. Hold on right there, buster.' And I did. I went back to my room and to this day I haven't smoked another cigarette."

He looked up at me. "But you know what I did? Every day I saved the exact amount of money I would have spent on cigarettes. Just as an experiment. Then last year I put it all together, and you know what I bought?"

I shook my head.

"I took that money and I bought a Nash Rambler."

My mother burst out laughing.

The principal sat back and smiled uncertainly. My mother was sniffing and searching in her purse. She found a Kleenex and blew her nose as if she had some kind of cold that made her shriek.

"Think about it," the principal said. "That's all I'm saying—just think about it."

My mother let the principal maunder on for a time, then brought him back to business. He became restless and uncomfortable. He said he would prefer that the vice-principal decide this question.

My mother refused. She told him that the the vice-principal had manhandled me while I was sick. The school nurse had seen him do it. If she had to, my mother said, she was prepared to talk to a lawyer. She didn't want to, but she would.

The principal saw no reason why it had to come to that. Not over one obscenity.

"He didn't do it," my mother said.

The principal tentatively, even reluctantly, mentioned the testimony of the weed fiends. My mother turned to me and asked if they were telling the truth.

"No ma'am."

"He doesn't lie to me," my mother said.

The principal was fidgeting. He seemed about ready to bolt. "Well," he said, "there is obviously some kind of confusion here."

My mother waited.

He looked from her to me and back to her. "What am I supposed to do? Just let it drop?" When she didn't answer he said, "All right. What about two weeks?"

"Two weeks what?"

"Suspension."

"Two weeks suspension?"

"One week, then. We'll split it. Does that seem fair?"

She frowned at the desk and said nothing.

He looked at her imploringly. "It's not that long. Just five days." Then he said, abruptly, "All right then, I'll let it go this time. That's fine for you," he added. "You don't have to work here."

School was over when we left the principal's office. We walked through the empty corridors, our footsteps echoing between long lines of lockers. I still had cramps. They got worse as I started moving around again, and on our way out I ducked into the lavatory. The janitor had already been there. He had changed what I'd written to BOCK YOU.

IT WAS TOO late for my mother to go back to work, so she went home early with me. Marian smelled a story and pressed my mother until she got it. We were sitting at the kitchen table, and as she listened to my mother Marian began looking back and forth between us and giving hard little shakes of her head as if to clear it of water. Then her eyes came to rest on me and did not move. When my mother came to the end, indignant all over again at the way I'd been treated, Marian asked me to leave them alone.

I listened from the living room. My mother argued at first but Marian overwhelmed her. This time, by God, she was going to make my mother see the light. Marian didn't have all the goods on me, but she had enough to keep her going for a while and she put her heart into it, hitting every note she knew in the song of my malfeasance.

It went on and on. I retreated upstairs to the bedroom and waited for my mother, rehearsing answers to the charges Marian had made against me. But when my mother came into the room she said nothing. She sat for a while on the edge of her bed, rubbing her eyes; then, moving slowly, she undressed to her slip and went into the bathroom and drew herself a bath, and lay in the water for a long time as she sometimes did when she got chilled coming home at night in a cold rain.

I had my answers ready but there were no questions. After my mother finished her bath she lay down and read, then fixed us dinner and read some more. She turned in early. Answers kept coming to me in the dark, proofs of my blamelessness that I knew to be false but could not stop myself from devising.

Dwight drove down that weekend. They spent a lot of time together, and finally my mother told me that Dwight was urging a proposal which she felt bound to consider. He proposed that after Christmas I move up to Chinook and live with him and go to school there. If things worked out, if I made a real effort and got along with him and his kids, she would quit her job and accept his offer of marriage.

She did not try to make any of this sound like great news. Instead she spoke as if she saw in this plan a duty which she would be selfish not to acknowledge. But first she wanted my approval. I thought I had no choice, so I gave it.

A Whole
New Deal

Dwight drove in a sullen reverie. When I spoke he answered curtly or not at all. Now and then his expression changed, and he grunted as if to claim some point of argument. He kept a Camel burning on his lower lip. Just the other side of Concrete he pulled the car hard to the left and hit a beaver that was crossing the road. Dwight said he had swerved to miss the beaver, but that wasn't true. He had gone out of his way to run over it. He stopped the car on the shoulder of the road and backed up to where the beaver lay.

We got out and looked at it. I saw no blood. The beaver was on its back with its eyes open and its curved yellow teeth bared. Dwight prodded it with his foot. "Dead," he said.

It was dead all right.

"Pick it up," Dwight told me. He opened the trunk of the car and said, "Pick it up. We'll skin the sucker out when we get home."

I wanted to do what Dwight expected me to do, but I couldn't. I stood where I was and stared at the beaver.

Dwight came up beside me. "That pelt's worth fifty dollars, bare minimum." He added, "Don't tell me you're afraid of the damned thing."

"No sir."

"Then pick it up." He watched me. "It's dead, for Christ's sake. It's just meat. Are you afraid of hamburger? Look." He bent down and gripped the tail in one hand and lifted the beaver off the ground. He tried to make this appear effortless but I could see he was surprised and strained by the beaver's weight. A stream of blood ran out of its nose, then stopped. A few drops fell on Dwight's shoes before he jerked the body away. Holding the beaver in front of him with both hands, Dwight carried it to the open trunk and let go. It landed hard. "There," he said, and wiped his hands on his pant leg.

We drove farther into the mountains. It was late afternoon. Pale cold light. The river flashed green through the trees beside the road, then turned gray as pewter when the sun dropped. The mountains darkened. Night came on.

Dwight stopped at a tavern in a village called Marblemount, the last settlement before Chinook. He brought a hamburger and fries out to the car and told me to sit tight for a while, then he went back inside. After I finished eating I put my coat on and waited for Dwight. Time passed, and more time. Every so often I got out of the car and walked short distances up and down the road. Once I risked a look through the tavern window but the glass was fogged up. I went back to the car and listened to the radio, keeping a sharp eye on the tavern door. Dwight had told me not to use the radio because it might wear down the battery. I still felt bad about being afraid of the beaver, and I didn't want to get in more trouble. I wanted everything to go just right.

I had agreed to move to Chinook partly because I thought I had no choice. But there was more to it than that. Unlike my mother, I was fiercely conventional. I was tempted by the idea of belonging to a conventional family, and living in a house, and having a big brother and a couple of sisters— especially if one of those sisters was Norma. And in my heart I despised the life I led in Seattle. I was sick of it and had no idea how to change it. I thought that in Chinook, away from Taylor and Silver, away from Marian, away from people who had already made up their minds about me, I could be different. I could introduce myself as a scholar-athlete, a boy of dignity and consequence, and without any reason to doubt me people would believe I was that boy, and thus allow me to be that boy. I recognized no obstacle to miraculous change but the incredulity of others. This was an idea that died hard, if it ever really died at all.

I played the radio softly, thinking I'd use less power that way. Dwight came out of the tavern a long time after he went in, at least as long a time as we'd spent getting there from Seattle, and gunned the car out of the lot. He drove fast, but I didn't worry until we hit a long series of curves and the car began to fishtail. This stretch of the road ran alongside a steep gorge; to our right the slope fell almost sheer to the river. Dwight sawed the wheel back and forth, seeming not to hear the scream of the tires. When I reached out for the dashboard he glanced at me and asked what I was afraid of now.

I said I was a little sick to my stomach.

"Sick to your stomach? A hotshot like you?"

The headlights slid off the road into darkness, then back again. "I'm not a hotshot," I said.

"That's what I hear. I hear you're a real hotshot. Come and go where you please, when you please. Isn't that right?"

I shook my head.

"That's what I hear," he said. "Regular man about town. Performer, too. That right? You a performer?"

"No sir."

"That's a goddamned lie." Dwight kept looking back and forth between me and the road.

"Dwight, please slow down," I said.

"If there's one thing I can't stomach," Dwight said, "it's a liar."

I pushed myself against the seat. "I'm not a liar."

"Sure you are. You or Marian. Is Marian a liar?" I didn't answer.

"She says you're quite the little performer. Is that a lie? You tell me that's a lie and we'll drive back to Seattle so you can call her a liar to her face. You want me to do that?"

I said no, I didn't.

"Then you must be the one that's the liar. Right?"

I nodded.

"Marian says you're quite the little performer. Is that true?"

"I guess," I said.

"You guess. You *guess*. Well, let's see your act. Go on. Let's see your act." When I didn't do anything, he said, "I'm waiting."

"I can't."

"Sure you can."

"No sir."

"Sure you can. Do me. I hear you do me."

I shook my head.

"Do me, I hear you're good at doing me. Do me with the lighter. Here. Do me with the lighter." He held out the Zippo in its velvet case. "Go on."

I sat where I was, both hands on the dashboard. We were all over the road.

"Take it!"

I didn't move.

He put the lighter back in his pocket. "Hotshot," he said. "You pull that hotshot stuff around me and I'll snatch you bald-headed, you understand?"

"Yes sir."

"You're in for a change, mister. You got that? You're in for a whole nother ball game."

I braced myself for the next curve.

Citizenship
in the Home

Dwight made a study of me. He thought about me during the day while he grunted over the engines of trucks and generators, and in the evening while he watched me eat, and late at night while he sat heavylidded at the kitchen table with a pint of Old Crow and a package of Camels to support him in his deliberations. He shared his findings as they came to him. The trouble with me was, I thought I was going to get through life without doing any work. The trouble with me was, I thought I was smarter than everyone else. The trouble with me was, I thought other people couldn't tell what I was thinking. The trouble with me was, I didn't think.

Another trouble with me was that I had too much free time. Dwight fixed that. He arranged for me to take over the local paper route. He had me join the Boy Scouts. He gave me a heavy load of chores, and encouraged Pearl to watch me and let him know if I was laggard or sloppy. Some of the chores were reasonable, some unreasonable, some bizarre as the meanest whims of a gnome setting tasks to a treasure seeker.

After Thanksgiving, once he knew I'd be coming to live with him, Dwight had filled several boxes with horse chestnuts from a stand of trees in front of the house, and now I was given the job of husking them. When Pearl and I finished the dinner dishes, Dwight would dump a pile of nuts on the floor of the utility room and put me to work with a knife and a pair of pliers until he judged that I'd done enough for the night. The husks were hard and covered with sharp spines. At first I wore gloves, but Dwight thought gloves were effeminate. He said that I needed bare hands to get a good grip on the husks, and on this point he was right, though he was wrong when he told me the spines weren't sharp enough to break skin. My fingers were crazed with cuts and scratches. Even worse, the broken husks bled a juice that made my hands stink and turned them orange. No amount of borax could get it off.

Except when Dwight had other plans for me I shucked horse chestnuts nearly every night, chipping away at them through most of the winter. I could have finished them off earlier but I slipped into daydreams and sat frozen like a kitchen boy in a spellbound castle, a nut in one hand, a tool in the other, until the sound of approaching footsteps woke me up and plunged me, blinking and confused, back into time.

The utility room lay just inside the front door. Utility room was Dwight's name for it; in other houses it was called the mud room. Everyone had to step around me and the horse chestnuts when leaving or entering the house, and on their way to the bathroom. Skipper nodded soberly each time he passed. Norma gave me sympathetic looks, and sometimes stopped for a moment to make insincere offers of help. Both of them let Dwight know they thought he was overdoing it. He told them to mind their own business. I kept hoping they'd really go to bat for me, but they had other things on their minds. Skipper was customizing his car. Norma was in love with Bobby Crow, an Indian boy from Marblemount who drove up almost every night to see her. Dwight disapproved of Bobby, but Norma slipped out of the house at will, and when Dwight bestirred himself to question her she fed him fat lies that he swallowed without a murmur. I knew where she and Bobby went; they went to the village dump, a petting zoo said to be frequented by a one-handed killer who had escaped from the state asylum at Sedro Woolley. Norma told me that one night she heard a noise outside the car and made Bobby lay rubber out of there. When they got back to the house they found a bloody hook hanging on the door handle. This was a true story that Norma made me promise never to tell anyone, ever. And there were bears at the dump, rooting in garbage and rearing up now and then with cans stuck on their noses.

As I worked my way through the horse chestnuts I took them up to the attic. This was a dank space where Pearl's old dolls were strewn, their eyes kindling under the glare of the flashlight, among broken appliances and stacks of *Collier's* and the washtub where the beaver lay curing in brine.

Skipper and Norma got used to seeing me with the nuts, because it was about the only way they ever saw me; their bus left for Concrete before I woke up in the morning and brought them back just in time for the evening meal. They came to accept the sight as normal. Pearl never got used to it. She passed my station twenty times a night on some pretext or other, lingering nearby until, in spite of myself, I raised my head and saw her looking down at me with hard bright eyes and a little smile. Sometimes Dwight came back to check on my progress. He tried to cheer me on with visions of everyone sitting together, a year or two down the line, eating these very nuts.

So I nodded away the nights over boxes of horse chestnuts, while my hands took on the color and glow of well-oiled baseball mitts. The smell grew deadly. The boys I went to school with were naturally obliged to shoot their mouths off, and finally—choosing the one I considered to be the weakest—I got into a fight. But by then the nuts were all husked anyway.

AFTER SCHOOL I delivered newspapers. Dwight had bought the route for almost nothing from a boy who was sick of it and couldn't find any other takers. I delivered the Seattle *Times* and the *Post-Intelligencer* to most of the houses in Chinook and to the barracks where the single men lived. The route paid between fifty and sixty dollars a month, money that Dwight took from me as soon as I collected it. He said that I would thank him someday, when I really needed the money.

I dawdled along the route, seizing any chance to delay going home. I sat in the bachelors' quarters and read their magazines (GENT GOES UNDERCOVER AT VASSAR! MY TEN YEARS AS A SEX-SLAVE OF THE AMAZONS OF THE WHITE NILE!). I fooled around with kids from school, played with dogs, read both papers front to back. Sometimes I just sat on a railing somewhere and looked up at the mountains.

They were always in shadow. The sun didn't make it up over the peaks before classes started in the morning, and it was gone behind the western rim by the time school let out. I lived in perpetual dusk.

The absence of light became oppressive to me. It took on the weight of other absences I could not admit to or even define but still felt sharply, on my own in this new place. My father and my brother. Friends. Most of all my mother, whose arrival seemed to grow more and more distant rather than closer. In the weeks since Christmas she had delayed giving Dwight a definite answer. She wanted to be sure, she told me. Marrying Dwight meant quitting her job, giving up the house, really burning her bridges. She couldn't rush into this one.

I understood, but understanding did not make me miss her less. She made the world seem friendly. And somehow, with her, it was. She would talk to anyone, anywhere, in grocery stores or ticket lines or restaurants, drawing them out and listening to their stories with intense concentration and partisan outbursts of sympathy. My mother did not expect to find people dull or mean; she assumed they would be likeable and interesting, and they felt this assurance, and mostly lived up to it. On the bus ride from Salt Lake to Portland she had everybody talking and laughing until it seemed like some kind of party. One of the passengers, a woman who owned a store in Portland, even offered her a job and a room in her house until we found a place of our own, an offer my mother declined because she had a lucky feeling about Seattle.

Now I saw her only when Dwight agreed to drive me down with him. He usually had reasons for leaving me behind, the paper route or schoolwork or something I had done wrong that week. But he had to bring me sometimes, and then he never let me out of his sight. He stuck close by and acted jovial. He smiled at me and put his hand on my shoulder and made frequent reference to fun things we'd done together. And I played along. Watching myself with revulsion, aghast at my own falsity yet somehow helpless to stop it, I simpered back at him and laughed when he invited me to laugh and confirmed all his lying implications that we were pals and our life together a good one. Dwight did this whenever it suited his purpose, and I never let him down. By the time our visits ended and my mother managed to get me alone for a moment, I was always so mired in pretense that I could see no way out. "How's it going?" she would ask, and I would answer, "Fine."

"For sure?"

"For sure."

We would be walking slowly toward the car, Dwight watching our approach. "If there's anything I should know, you tell me. Okay?"

"Yes ma'am."

"Promise."

I would promise. And then I would get in the car with Dwight and he would drive me back to the mountains, smoking, brooding, looking over at me to see if he could catch some expression on my face that would give me away and explain why my mother kept putting off her decision. When we reached Marblemount he would stop at the tavern and drink for a couple of hours, then take me through the turns above the river and tell me some more things that were wrong with me.

Dwight's bill of particulars contained some truth. But it went on and on. It never ended, and before long it lost its power to hurt me. I experienced it as more bad weather to get through, not biting, just close and dim and heavy.

I walked my paper route at glacial speed, the news bag swinging against my chest and back. I sat on my customers' steps, staring off at nothing. I did multiplication tables in my head. I dreamed of doing brave, selfless deeds, generally of a military character; dreamed them so elaborately that I knew the histories of my comrades, saw their faces, heard their voices, felt grief when my heroism was insufficient to save them. As the dusk turned to night Dwight would send Pearl out with messages for me: Dad says you better get a move on, or else. Dad says hustle your buns, or else.

ONE NIGHT A week I went to Boy Scout meetings. To make sure that I wouldn't just play grab-ass at the meetings but really do some serious scouting, as he had done when he was my age, Dwight signed up as Assistant Scoutmaster. He gave me an outsize uniform that Skipper had once worn. For himself he bought a new uniform and all the accoutrements. Unlike the Scoutmaster, who wore jeans and sneakers with his regulation shirt, Dwight came to every meeting in the full plumage of insignia and braid and scarves, wearing shoes that I had spit-shined as he looked on to point out spots I'd missed or brought to an imperfect luster. While the Scoutmaster ran the meetings Dwight stood against the wall or chatted with the older boys, smoking and laughing at their jokes. We always left the meetings together, like father and son, smiling and waving good-bye, then walked home in silence.

As soon as we got home, Dwight sat down at the kitchen table with a glass of Old Crow and reviewed my performance. I hadn't paid attention during the announcements. I'd spent too much time goofing off with the wrong boys. I'd forgotten to check for the tongue during artificial respiration. Why couldn't I remember that? *Check for the goddam tongue!* I could work on some poor drowned sonofabitch till the cows came home but it wasn't going to do squat for him if he'd swallowed his tongue. Was that so hard to remember?

And I would say No, next time I'd remember, but the truth was I hadn't forgotten at all, I just didn't want to put my fingers in some kid's mouth after he'd been eating peanut butter and crackers. If I ever came across an actual drowned person I would do everything I was supposed to do, even the business with the tongue; I just couldn't perform solemn and efficient resuscitation upon the body of a boy who was whispering that his pud was waterlogged and in need of a big squeeze.

But I liked being a Scout. I was stirred by the elevated diction in which we swore our fealty to the chaste chivalric fantasies of Lord Baden-Powell. My uniform, baggy and barren though it was, made me feel like a soldier. I became a serious student of the ranks and honors available to the ambitious, and made up calenders of deadlines by which I planned my rise from Tenderfoot to Eagle. I developed a headwaiter's eye; when we met with other troops to compete at Scout skills I could read their uniforms at a glance and know exactly who was who. The main purpose of scouting as I understood it was to accumulate symbols that would compel respect, or at least civility, from those who shared them and envy from those who did not. Conspicuous deeds of patriotism and piety, rope craft, water wisdom, fire wizardry, first-aid, all the arts of forest and mountain and stream, seemed to me just different ways of getting badges.

Dwight gave me Skipper's old Scout manual, *Handbook for Boys*, outdated even when Skipper had it, a 1942 edition full of pictures of "Fighting Scouts" keeping a lookout for Nazi subs and Jap bombers. I read the *Handbook* almost every night, cruising for easy merit badges like Indian Lore, Bookbinding, Reptile Study, and Personal Health ("Show proper method of brushing teeth and discuss the importance of dental care. . . ."). The merit-badge index was followed by advertisements for official Scout gear, and then a list of The Firms That Make the Things You Want, among them Coca-Cola, Eastman Kodak, Evinrude and Nestle's ("The Boy Scout Emergency Ration"), and finally by a section called Where to Go to School. The schools were mostly military academies with sonorous double-barreled names. Carson Long. Morgan Park. Cochran-Bryan. Valley Forge. Castle Heights.

I liked reading all these advertisements. They were a natural part of the *Handbook*, in whose pages the Scout Spirit and the spirit of commerce mingled freely, and often indistinguishably. "What the Scout *Is* determines his progress in whatever line of business he may seek success—and Scout Ideals mean progress in business." Suggested good turns were enumerated on a ledger, so the Scout could check them off as he performed them: *Assisted a foreign boy with some English grammar. Helped put out a burning field. Gave water to crippled dog.* Here, even the murky enterprise of self-examination could be expressed as a problem in accounting. "On a scale of 100, what all-around rating would I be justified in giving myself?"

I liked all these numbers and lists, because they offered the clear possibility of mastery. But what I liked best about the *Handbook* was its voice, the bluff hail-fellow language by which it tried to make being a good boy seem adventurous, even romantic. The Scout Spirit was traced to King Arthur's Round Table, and from there to the explorers and pioneers and warriors whose conquests had been achieved through fair play and clean living. "No man given over to dissipation can stand the gaff. He quickly tires. He is the type who usually lacks courage at the crucial moment. He cannot take punishment and come back smiling."

I yielded easily to this comradely tone, forgetting while I did so that I was not the boy it supposed I was.

Boy's Life, the official Scout magazine, worked on me in the same way. I read it in a trance, accepting without question its narcotic invitation to believe that I was really no different from the boys whose hustle and pluck it celebrated. Boys who raised treasure from Spanish galleons, and put empty barns to use by building operational airplanes in them. Boys who skied to the North Pole. Boys who sailed around the Horn, solo. Boys who saved lives, and were accepted into savage tribes, and sent themselves to college by running traplines in the wilderness. Reading about these boys made me restless, feverish with schemes.

My mother had allowed me to bring the Winchester to Chinook. When I was alone in the house I sometimes dressed up in my Scout uniform, slung the rifle across my back, and practiced Indian sign language in front of the mirror.

Hungry.

Brother.

Food.

Want.

Great Mystery.

MY MOTHER FINALLY gave Dwight a date in March. Once he knew she was coming he began to talk about his plans for renovating the house, but he drank at night and didn't get anything done. A couple of weeks before she quit her job he brought home a trunkful of paint in five-gallon cans. All of it was white. Dwight spread out his tarps and for several nights running we stayed up late painting the ceilings and walls. When we had finished those, Dwight looked around, saw that it was good, and kept going. He painted the coffee table white. He painted all the beds white, and the chests of drawers, and the dining-room table. He called it "blond" when he put it on the furniture, but it wasn't blond or even off-white; it was stark, industrial strength, eye-frying white. The house reeked of oil.

My mother called a few days before Dwight was supposed to drive down and pick her up. She talked to him for a while, then asked to speak to me. She wanted to know how I was.

Okay, I told her.

She said she had been feeling kind of low and just wanted to check with me, make sure I felt good about everything. It was such a big step. Were Dwight and I getting along all right?

I said we were. He was in the living room with me, painting some chairs, but I probably would have given the same answer if I'd been alone.

My mother told me she could still change her mind. She could keep her job and find another place to live. I understood, didn't I, that it wasn't too late?

I said I did, but I didn't. I had come to feel that all of this was fated, that I was bound to accept as my home a place I did not feel at home in, and to take as my father a man who was offended by my existence and would never stop questioning my right to it. I did not believe my mother when she told me it wasn't too late. I knew she meant what she said, but it seemed to me that she was deceiving herself. Things had gone too far. And somehow it was her telling me it wasn't too late that made me believe, past all doubt, that it was. Those words still sound to me less like a hope than an epitaph, the last lic we tell before hurling ourselves over the brink.

After my mother hung up, Dwight and I finished painting the dining-room chairs. Then he lit a cigarette and looked around, his brush still in his hands. He gazed pensively at the piano. He said, "Sort of stands out, doesn't it?"

I looked at it with him. It was an old Baldwin upright, cased in black walnut, that he had bought for twenty dollars from a family on the move who'd grown tired of hauling it around. Dwight did a victory dance after bringing it home. He said the stupid compones had no idea what it was worth, that it was worth twice that much. Dwight sat down at it one night with the idea of demonstrating his virtuosity, but after making a few sour chords he slammed it shut and pronounced it out of tune. He never went near it again. Sometimes Pearl banged out "Chopsticks" but otherwise it got no play at all. It was just a piece of furniture, so dark in all this whiteness that it seemed to be pulsing. You really couldn't look anywhere else.

I agreed that it stood out.

We went to work on it. Using fine bristles so our brush strokes wouldn't show, we painted the bench, the pedestal, the fluted columns that rose from the pedestal to the keyboard. We painted the carved scrollwork. We painted the elaborate inlaid picture above the keyboard, a picture of a girl with braided yellow hair leaning out of her gabled window to listen to a redbird on a branch. We painted the lustrous cabinet. We even painted the foot pedals. Finally, because the antique yellow of the ivory looked wrong to Dwight against the new white, we very carefully painted the keys, all except the black ones, of course.

I was standing on the road with two other boys, my news bag still heavy with papers, when I saw him coming toward us with his little dog, Pepper. The three of us started making cracks about him. His name was Arthur Gayle and he was the uncoolest boy in the sixth grade, maybe even the whole camp. Arthur was a sissy. His mother was said to have turned him into a sissy by dressing him in girls' clothes when he was little. He walked like a girl, ran like a girl, and threw like a girl. Arthur was my father's name, so that seemed okay to me, but the name Gayle implicated him further in sissyhood. He was clever. He had an arch, subtle voice that he used to good effect as an instrument of his cleverness. I'd come away smarting from all my exchanges with him.

Arthur was testy with me. He seemed to want something. At times I caught him looking at me expectantly, as if I were holding out on him. And I was. All my life I have recognized almost at a glance those who were meant to be my friends, and they have recognized me. Arthur was one of these. I liked him. I liked his acid wit and the wild stories he told and his apparent indifference to what other people thought of him. But I had withheld my friendship, because I was afraid of what it would cost me.

As Arthur came toward us he set his face in a careless smirk. He must have known we were talking about him. Instead of walking past, he turned to me and said, "Didn't your momma teach you to wash your hands after you go pee?"

My hands weren't all that yellow anymore, in fact they were nearly back to normal. I'd finished shucking the nuts weeks before.

It was springtime. The earth was spongy with melted snow, and on the warmest days, if you listened for it, you could hear a faint steady sibilance of evaporation, almost like a light rain. The trees were hazy with new growth. Bears had begun to appear on the glistening granite faces of the mountainsides above us, taking the sun and soaking up heat from the rock; at lunchtime people came out onto their steps and watched them with upturned, benevolent faces. My mother was with me again. The nuts were all husked and drying in the attic. What did I need trouble for?

I was inclined to let it go. But I didn't like being laughed at, and I didn't like comments about my hands. Arthur had made other such comments. He was bigger than me, especially around the middle, but I factored out this weight as blubber. I could take him, I felt sure. I had provocation, and I had witnesses to carry the news. It seemed like a good time to make a point.

I started things off by calling him Fatso.

Arthur continued to smile at me. "Excuse me," he said, "but has anyone ever told you that you look exactly like a pile of wet vomit?"

We went on like this, and then I called him a sissy.

The smile left his face. And at that moment it came to me that although everyone referred to Arthur as a sissy, I had never heard anyone actually use the word in front of him. And in the same moment, seeing how everything about him changed after the word was spoken, how suddenly red and awful his face became, I understood that there must be a reason for this. A crucial bit of history I should have known about, and didn't.

His first swing caught me dead on the ear. There was an explosion inside my head, then a continuous rustling sound as of someone crumpling paper. It lasted for days. When he swung again I turned away and took his fist on the back of my head. He threw punches the way he threw balls, sidearm, with a lot of wrist, but he somehow got his weight behind them before they landed. This one knocked me to my knees. He drew back his foot and kicked me in the stomach. The papers in my bag deadened the blow but I was stunned by the fact that he had kicked me at all. I saw that his commitment to this fight was absolute.

His dog barked in my face.

When I got up Arthur rushed me, arms flailing, fists raining on my shoulders. He almost knocked me down again but I surprised us both by landing one on his eye. He stopped and roared. The eye was already closing up, his face gone scarlet, his nostrils streaming gouts of snot. When I saw his eye I got worried. I was ready to stop, but he wasn't. He flew at me again. I closed with him and got him in a hug to keep his arms still. We staggered over the road like drunken dancers, and then he hooked my leg and tripped me and we rolled off the shoulder and down the long muddy embankment, both of us flailing and kicking with our knees and screaming gibberish in each other's ears. He had gone insane, I could see that, and it seemed to me that my only chance was to go insane too.

Still rolling, we hit the boggy swale at the foot of the bank. He got on top of me, I got on top of him, he got back on top of me. My news bag had armored me well when I was on my feet but now it was heavy with mud and twisted around my shoulders. I couldn't get off a good swing. All I could do was hold on to Arthur and try to keep him from getting one off at me. He struggled, then abruptly collapsed on top of me. He was panting for breath. His weight pressed me into the mud. I gathered myself and bucked him off. It took everything I had. We lay next to each other, gasping strenuously. Pepper tugged at my pant leg and growled.

Arthur stirred. He got to his feet and started up the bank. I followed him, thinking it was all over, but when he got to the top he turned and said, "Take it back."

The other boys were watching me. I shook my head.

Arthur pushed me and I began sliding down the bank. "Take it back," he yelled.

Pepper followed me in my descent, yapping and lunging. There hadn't been a moment since the fight began when Pepper wasn't worrying me in some way, if only to bark and bounce around me, and finally it was this more than anything else that made me lose heart. It wounded my spirit to have a dog against me. I *liked* dogs. I liked dogs more than I liked people, and I expected them to like me back.

I started up the bank again, Pepper still at my heels.

"Take it back," Arthur said.

"Okay," I said.

"Say it."

"Okay. I take it back."

"No. Say, 'You're not a sissy.'"

I looked up at him and the other two boys. There was pleasure and scorn on their faces, but not on his. He wore, instead, an expression of such earnestness that it seemed impossible to refuse him what he asked. I said, "You're not a sissy."

He called Pepper and turned away. When I got to the top he was walking toward home. The other two boys were excited, restless, twitching with the blows they'd imagined striking. They wanted to talk about the fight, but I had lost interest in it. My clothes were caked with mud. My news bag, full of mud and ruined papers, pulled down on me. My ear hurt.

I trudged homeward.

Pearl was sitting on the steps, eating something. She looked me over as I walked up. "You're in Dutch," she said.

MY MOTHER HAD me undress in the utility room and take a shower. Then she sat me down in the kitchen and dabbed iodine on some scratches I'd picked up, probably from rolling around on the road. She tried to be severe. I knew she

123

wasn't angry, but I also knew she would become angry if I did not produce some mimicry of remorse, so I hung my head and declared that I would certainly think twice before letting myself be goaded into another fight. "You better tell Dad," Pearl said to my mother.

My mother nodded wearily. "You can tell him," she said.

She and Dwight weren't getting along. They hadn't gotten along since the night they returned from their honeymoon in Vancouver, two days early, silent and grim, not even looking at each other as they carried the suitcases into the house and down the hall to Dwight's room. That night Dwight sat up drinking and went to sleep on the sofa. He did this often, sometimes three or four nights in a row, weekends especially. I was always the first one up on Saturday and Sunday because the papers came in early on those days, and when I got up I usually found Dwight asleep on the sofa, a test pattern hissing on the TV.

For the first few weeks my mother was utterly cast down. She slept late, something she had never done before, and when I came home for lunch I sometimes found her still in her bathrobe, sitting at the kitchen table and staring dazedly down the bright white tunnel of the house. I had never seen my mother give up. I hadn't even known the possibility existed, but now I knew, and it gave me pause. It made me feel for a little while the truth that everything good in my life could be lost, that it was all drawn day by day from someone else's store of hope and will. But my mother got better, and I found other things to think about.

She did not give up. Instead, she chose to believe that she could still make a life in Chinook. She joined the PTA and persuaded the head of the rifle club to admit her as a member. She took a part-time job waitressing in the bachelors' mess hall. She filled the house with plants, mothered Pearl, and insisted that all of us spend time together like a real family.

And so we did. But our failure was ordained, because the real family we set out to imitate does not exist in nature; a real family as troubled as ours would never dream of spending time together.

Dwight thought that most of these troubles were my fault. And a lot of them were. I screwed up constantly, even when I meant to do well. Every screwup was good for a scene, and this fight I'd gotten into with Arthur Gayle was going to be good for a big one.

When the whistle blew at five o'clock Pearl went outside to wait for Dwight.

HE CAME STRAIGHT to my room. When the door opened behind me I stared at the homework on my desk and prepared a bland, innocent face. I turned and presented it to him. He was grinning. He crossed the room and sat on Skipper's bed. Still grinning, he said, "Who won?"

He had me tell the story again and again. Each time I told it he laughed and slapped his leg. I began by admitting, reluctantly, that I might have started the fight by calling Arthur a sissy; then, seeing how much pleasure it gave Dwight to hear this, I recalled that my actual words were "big fat sissy." I told him I'd knocked Arthur down and I described his swollen eye. I allowed Dwight to think that I had kicked some very serious ass that day.

"You actually gave him a black eye?" Dwight said.

"Well, it wasn't black *yet.*"

"But it was all puffed up?"

I nodded.

"Then it's a shiner," he said. "For sure."

I hedged the big question, the question of who had won. I let on that my victory had been less than decisive because Arthur had hit me in the ear when I wasn't expecting it.

"That was your fault," Dwight told me. "You must have had your guard down. There's no excuse for getting dry-gulched." He started pacing the room. "I can show you a couple of moves that'll leave little lord Gayle wondering what month he's in."

At dinner that night Dwight had me repeat the story to Skipper and Norma, and then he told a story of his own. "When I was your age," he said, "there was a kid who used to sit behind me in school and lip off all the time. He had what I call diarrhea of the mouth. Well, he lipped off just once too often and I told him to shut up. Oh yeah? he says. Who's gonna make me? I am, I tell him. Oh yeah? he says. You and who else's army? Just the three of us, I say. Me, myself, and I.

"Well, after school that day he waits across the street with this friend of his and as soon as I come out of the building he yells something. I guess he thought I was just going to go home and forget about it. But I'll tell you something. With people like that, you've got to hurt them, you've got to inflict pain. It's the only thing they understand. Otherwise you've got them on your back for good. Believe me, I'm speaking from experience.

"Okay. It was really cold out, really freezing. There were these frozen horse turds lying all over the place—road apples, we called them. So I picked one up and went over to this guy, but not acting tough, okay? *Not acting tough.* Acting more like, Oh gee, I'm so scared, please don't hurt me. Sort of like this." Dwight slumped his shoulders and dropped his chin and simpered up from beneath his eyebrows.

"So I came over to him and in this little scaredy-cat voice I say, Excuse me, what's the problem? He of course starts in on me again, blah blah blah, and while he's got his mouth open *I jam a road apple into it!* You should've seen the look on his face. Then I hit the sucker in the breadbasket, and down he goes. I sit on him for a while and hold my hand over his mouth until the road apple starts melting, then I get up and leave him there. I caught holy hell for it later on, but so what."

After dinner Dwight took me into the utility room and showed me some moves. He taught me how to stand and shuffle my feet and guard myself. He showed me how to throw a punch from the shoulder instead of winding up and leaving myself open. Then he showed me how to dry-gulch somebody. It wasn't a thing I should do casually, Dwight said, but only if I had good reason to think that the other fellow might dry-gulch me. There were many techniques but Dwight didn't want to confuse me, so he showed me two of the best.

It was simple, really. You just walked up to someone and acted friendly or even scared, then you kicked him in the balls. That was the first technique. The second was almost exactly the same, except that instead of kicking the other guy in the balls you punched him in the windpipe. According to Dwight this worked best on tall guys. We practiced both moves. Dwight had me approach him nonchalantly, say "Hello," and then kick or swing. At first I was afraid he would use these maneuvers as an excuse to cream me—all in the spirit of serious training, of course. But he didn't. He caught my fist or foot almost gently, let go, spoke a few words of correction, and told me to try again. He was quick and strong, and enjoyed watching me realize it.

Feet squeaking on the floor, faces shiny with sweat, we worked out until I had the moves down cold. Then we went back into the kitchen. Dwight had a drink and gave me tips about dealing with Arthur: how I should bide my time, and make sure we were alone, and not give him any warning, and so on. I saw that he considered this to be my right and my duty. Bide your time, he told me.

A few people called that night to complain about their missing newspapers. Dwight took the calls and explained that the papers had been ruined in a fight, adding that his boy Jack had hung a real shiner on the Gayle kid.

*   *   *

I HAD, TOO. Arthur's eye did not immediately turn black, but first went through a liverish spectrum of yellows and purples and greens. Arthur sometimes stared at me in a way that convinced me he knew I'd been telling lies about the fight. But he made no move to start it up again. We kept away from each other. Once school let out for the summer, we hardly ever met except in a crowd of other boys at baseball games and Scout meetings.

But one afternoon I was doing my route and saw Arthur coming toward me down the main road. We would meet each other not far from where the fight had started. There was no one else around. I walked on and so did he, Pepper mincing along behind him. And as we approached each other it occurred to me, more as nervousness than thought, that Arthur might also have received some instruction in dry-gulching, and in biding his time. I had bided my own beyond Dwight's patience, that was for sure.

When we were close enough to touch, Arthur stopped and said, "Hi."

"Hi," I said.

We stood there, looking at each other. Then he looked down at Pepper. "Do you want to pet my dog?" he asked.

"Sure." I dropped to one knee and held out my hand. Pepper sniffed it.

"She can talk," Arthur said.

"Sure," I said. "I just about believe you."

"Hey, Pepper," he said, "what's on a tree?"

She yapped twice.

"Bark!" Arthur said. "Way to go, Pepper. Okay, Pepper, how's the world treating you?"

She looked up at him.

"How's the world treating you, Pepper?"

She yapped again.

"Rough! Good girl!"

It was a dumb joke, but I had to laugh. While I stroked Pepper's wiry fur she grunted softly and looked up at me with keen, unremembering eyes.

Skipper's car was a 1949 Ford that Dwight had gotten a deal on from some rube in Marblemount. Dwight bought it so Skipper could take girls out and go hunting and fishing without borrowing his own car, but Skipper put it in a corrugated iron shed at the edge of camp and commenced taking it to pieces. It had been in pieces for over a year when I moved up to Chinook, and it was still in pieces six months later when Skipper graduated from Concrete High.

Skipper didn't leave Chinook when he graduated, but took a job with the power company and continued living at home so he could put all his money into the car. Sometimes at night I dropped by to look at it while I was out collecting from my subscribers. At home Skipper took little notice of me, but in the shed he became hospitable. He turned off whatever tool he happened to be plying at the time and raised his goggles to his forehead. He gave me Cokes to drink while he explained what the various parts of the car were and what he planned to do with them. I nodded as if I understood, and really believed that one day this mess would put itself together again.

Though Skipper was supposed to start at the University of Washington in September, he didn't give any sign of leaving. Dwight began to ride him. He wanted to know where

Skipper expected to live, and how he was going to pay for his education. He wanted to know what the plan was. Skipper said he had it all worked out.

Dwight kept at him, but Skipper just smiled his polite uninterested smile and did as he pleased. And then, late that summer, the car began to come together just as Skipper had said it would. I was in the shed the night he and his friends put the rebuilt engine in. Skipper had installed racing carbs and bored out the cylinders to make it more powerful, then he'd had it chromed. It was beautiful. His friends wrestled it in with a block and tackle while Skipper shouted orders at them, and within an hour he had it roaring.

The body looked beyond saving. It was dented, dull, and full of holes from the ornaments Skipper had stripped off. He leaded in the holes, fiberglassed the dents, laid on a coat of primer, sanded it smooth, and put on sixteen coats of candy-apple red lacquer paint. He fine-sanded each coat before adding the next. It took him over a month, and by the time he was done the paint had such clarity and depth it was like looking into a glaze of thick red ice. The lines of the car were fluid, clean; he had been right to take off the ornaments.

Once the painting was done Skipper put on new white-wall tires with chrome hubcaps, not the flipper hubcaps that were in fashion then but simple globes as bright as mirrors. Along the sides, under the doors, he hung chrome Laker exhaust pipes that bent out slightly at the end as if to cough the smoke discreetly away from the car. He put a rechromed bumper in front and attached a Continental kit to the rear end—an unusually long bumper with an external case for the spare tire.

It was cherry. The only thing that needed fixing was the interior. Skipper told me he had just enough money left to take the car down to Tijuana and have it upholstered there. He was going to have it done in white leather, tucked, rolled, and pleated.

When I asked him if I could come along he told me he'd think about it.

I thought he was serious. I thought that he would actually consider taking me with him, and since I could imagine no reasonable argument against my going I assumed that he couldn't either. It was as good as decided. I saw myself riding shotgun beside Skipper in this fast, beautiful red car, the two of us having adventures along the way and helping people out of situations too tough for them to handle by themselves. They would want us to stay afterward but we would always move on, leaving them to stare at our dust as we receded down the highway. It seemed to me that Mexico, a barren place with unseen trumpet players wandering in the background, was a long way off, and that we would be a long time gone.

I told Arthur I was going. I also told a few other kids, and some of the people on my paper route. As we were eating dinner one night Dwight said, "Say there, mister, what's this I hear about you going to Mexico?" He was looking at me.

Pearl said, "If he gets to go, I get to go too."

My mother laughed. "Mexico! Who said anything about Mexico?"

"He did," Dwight told her.

"Jack, is that true?" my mother asked. "Did you tell someone you were going to Mexico?"

"Skipper said I could," I told her.

"Huh?" Skipper said. "I said *what?*"

I looked at him and remembered for the first time in
days that he hadn't actually said I could go along. "You said
you'd think about it," I told him.

"No kidding? I said that?"

I nodded.

"Solly, Cholly," he said. "No can do." He must have seen
the effect these words had on me, because he went on to explain that his friend Ray was planning to go along. They'd be
sleeping in the car to save money and that meant there was
only room for the two of them.

"It's a moot point," Dwight said. *It's a moot point* was
one of his favorite weighty utterances, that and *It's academic.*

"Some other time," Skipper said.

Pearl asked him to get her a sombrero.

"I want castanets," Norma said. She wiggled her shoulders and sang "La Cucaracha" until Dwight told her to pipe
down.

SKIPPER AND I shared the smallest room in the house. We used
the same desk, the same dresser, the same closet. A space of
five or six feet separated our beds. But I never felt cramped
in there until Skipper left for Mexico. Because he took up so

much room when he was home, I could not forget that he was gone, and that led me to think about him and his friend Ray out on the road, free as birds. And those thoughts made me feel cheated and confined. I believed that Skipper should have taken me instead of Ray. I had asked first and, after all, I was his brother. This meant something to me but I saw that it meant nothing to him. I hadn't always gotten along with my own brother, and we hadn't even seen each other in four years, but I still missed him and began to imagine how much better he would treat me.

I also missed my father. My mother never complained to me about him, but sometimes Dwight would make sarcastic comments about Daddy Warbucks and Lord High-and-Mighty. He meant to impugn my father for being rich and living far away and having nothing to do with me, but all these qualities, even the last, perhaps especially the last, made my father fascinating. He had the advantage always enjoyed by the inconstant parent, of not being there to be found imperfect. I could see him as I wanted to see him. I could give him sterling qualities and imagine good reasons, even romantic reasons, why he had taken no interest, why he had never written to me, why he seemed to have forgotten I existed. I made excuses for him long after I should have known better. Then, when I did know better, I resolved to put the fact of his desertion from my mind. I visited him on my way to Vietnam, and then again when I got back, and we became friends. He was no monster—he'd had troubles of his own. Anyway, only crybabies groused about their parents.

This way of thinking worked pretty well until my first child was born. He came three weeks early, when I was away from home. The first time I saw him, in the hospital nursery, a nurse was trying to take a blood sample from him. She couldn't find a vein. She kept jabbing him, and every time the needle went in I felt it myself. My impatience made her so clumsy that another nurse had to take over. When I finally got my hands on him I felt as if I had snatched him from a pack of wolves, and as I held him something hard broke in me, and I knew that I was more alive than I had been before. But at the same time I felt a shadow, a coldness at the edges. It made me uneasy, so I ignored it. I didn't understand what it was until it came upon me again that night, so sharply I wanted to cry out. It was about my father, ten years dead by then. It was grief and rage, mostly rage, and for days I shook with it when I wasn't shaking with joy for my son, and for the new life I had been given.

But that was still to come. As a boy, I found no fault in my father. I made him out of dreams and memories. One of these memories was of sitting in the kitchen of my stepmother's beautiful old house in Connecticut, where I had come for a visit, and watching him unload a box full of fireworks onto the table. It was all heavy ordnance, seriously life-threatening and illegal. My stepmother was scolding him. She wanted to know what he planned to do with them. He pushed a bunch of cherry bombs over to me and said, "Blow 'em up, dear, blow 'em up."

* * *

I BEGAN TO take a sharp, acquisitive interest in cars after Skipper customized the Ford. As I walked my paper route I took apart the cars I saw and put them back together in more interesting ways, lowered, louvered, dagoed, chopped-and-channeled. I read the used-car advertisements in the papers, comparing prices, measuring them against the money I was making. I thought of what it would be like to own a car, to be able to just get in and go.

After I'd delivered my papers one day I folded up my news bag and crossed the bridge leading out of camp, then waited with my thumb in the air until a car stopped for me. I didn't know the man—he was a construction worker from the dam upriver. I got in and he asked me where I was going. He added, "You're good as far as Seattle. Then you're on your own."

Seattle. I could, if I chose, ride all the way to Seattle. I said that I was going to Concrete, which seemed far enough for now, but by the time we reached Marblemount I lost my nerve and asked the man to let me out. Within moments I caught another ride back to Chinook. This was my first time hitchhiking. As the summer went on I ranged farther and farther down the valley, to Concrete and Bird's Eye and Van Horn and Sedro Woolley; once, just before school started, all the way to Mount Vernon. I would walk around the streets of these towns for a few minutes, waiting for something to happen, and when it didn't I would go back to the road and stick my thumb out again. I was always home by the time Dwight and my mother got off work. No one ever missed me. Now and then I went with Arthur, but usually alone. Alone I could lie more freely and I felt more open to chance. Someday, I thought, someone would stop for me and say, "You're good as far as Wilton, Connecticut . . ."

SKIPPER WAS AWAY for only a couple of weeks. He came back, packed up his things, and was gone the next morning. I saw him occasionally after that, when he came home for Thanksgiving and Christmas or when we visited him in Seattle. He lived in little apartments with other men for a couple of years, then he got married and took another job with the power company. I sat around with him the night before his wedding. It was one of two times I ever saw him choked up. In this case the emotion was brought on not by the prospect of losing his freedom but by a song he kept playing on his new hi-fi—"The Everglades," by the Kingston Trio. It told the story of a man who kills another man in a fight over a woman. Seeing what he has done, he takes to the glades,

> *Where a man can hide, and never be found*
> *And have no fear of the bayin' hound*
> *But he better keep movin' and don't stand still*
> *'Cause if the skeeters don't get him then the 'gators will*

What the man doesn't know, and of course will never find out, is that the jury has acquitted him on grounds of self-defense. This kicker is revealed in the last verse, and every time it came around Skipper lowered his eyes and shook his head mournfully.

The other time I saw him choked up was when he got back from Mexico. We were eating dinner. The sound of the engine was unmistakable, and when we heard it Pearl and Norma and I jumped up and ran outside. Dwight and my mother followed a moment later. The family that shared our building came outside too, and so did some other neighbors, all of them struck speechless by the sight of the car.

It looked as if it had been sandblasted. The paint was pitted and dull. The hubcaps and bumpers and Laker pipes were also pitted, and beginning to rust. It was a sad sight.

Skipper told us what had happened. After he had the car upholstered he and Ray took a run down to Ensenada, and on the way back they got caught in a sandstorm. The sand was so thick they couldn't see more than a foot or two in front of them. They'd had to pull off the road and wait it out, which took the best part of a day. The sand fouled the engine, too—Skipper had been tinkering with it all the way home. He made jokes about the whole episode but his voice was close to breaking. He'd been holding it in all this time, probably putting up a show of nonchalance for Ray, but now the sight of his home and family was unmanning him. He did not break down, but he was close to it.

While Skipper talked I circled the car, toting up the damage. I opened the driver's door and poked my head inside. The floor had been carpeted in white. White leather covered the seats, side panels, roof and dashboard. The light inside was rich and creamy. I got in behind the wheel and closed the door. I breathed in the smell of the leather. I ran my fingers over the seats, then leaned back with one hand on the wheel and the other on the gear shift. Softly, so no one would hear me, I made engine noises and worked the gears, looking through the pitted windshield at the blurry outline of the trees along the road. If I didn't look too hard I could almost believe I was moving.

I kept outgrowing my shoes, two pairs in the seventh grade alone. Dwight was indignant. He thought I was growing out of malice. He put off buying the third pair until I could hardly walk, and said there would be no sneakers this time. We would talk about sneakers when I settled down and decided what size my feet were going to be. I wanted to buy them myself out of my savings from the paper route, but Dwight refused to withdraw the money from the bank.

I wouldn't have cared that much about the sneakers except for basketball. The Chinook grade school had very few boys to draw on for sports, which meant that I got to play in most of the games, and wear a sharp uniform—red satin with white stripes. I was not wrong to suppose that this uniform would lose a certain something with the addition of brown street shoes.

We played our games at night. When they were away my mother usually drove me, but if she was busy Norma would get Bobby Crow to take me in his car. Of course Norma came along too. This was one of their ways to steal time together. On the drive to the game Bobby gave me tips, inside dope about passing, shooting, feinting. I hung over the front seat as Bobby talked, nodding shrewdly at everything he said. Bobby had played football for Concrete High. He'd been their quarter-back, the smallest and best player on the team, so much better than the others that he seemed alone on the field. His solitary excellence made him beautiful and tragic, because you knew that whatever prodigies he performed would be undone by the rest of the team. He made sly, unseen handoffs to butterfin-gered halfbacks, long bull's-eye passes to ends who couldn't catch them. But his true wizardry was brokenfield running: sprinting and stopping dead, jumping sideways, pirouetting on his toes and wriggling his hips girlishly as he spun away from the furious hulks who pursued him, slipping between them like a trout shooting down a boulder-strewn creek.

Bobby was small-boned and slender. He neither drank nor smoked. He had the narrow features of his half-caste mother and the dark eyes and skin of his Nez Percé father, who, Norma told me, was a direct descendant of Chief Joseph. Bobby did not play basketball for Concrete, but I listened to all his words of advice and squeezed my mind around them so they would sink in deep and change my game. Bobby had a very soft voice, and this made what he said seem confidential, even a little shady.

I PLAYED MY first game in street shoes against Van Horn. Bobby and Norma let me off outside the school and drove away. They had been glum and prickly with each other on the way down. In a few months they'd be graduating, and their plans didn't agree.

I knew I was in trouble as soon as we started our layup drills. The shoes were heavy and squarish, chosen by Dwight to go with both my school clothes and my Scout uniform. They clomped loudly as I ran and the slick new soles slipped like skates on the profoundly varnished floor. I fell down twice before the game began. By tip-off the kids from the other school were already hooting at me. I didn't want to play, but only five of us had shown up that night so I had no choice. My shoes clomped as I ran blindly up and down the court. Sometimes the ball came at me. I dribbled it once or twice and threw it at someone else in red. Jumped when I saw everyone else jumping. Ran back and forth. Fell down whenever I tried to stop too fast.

In the din of voices I heard one in particular, a woman's, shrieking high above the rest. It was like the crazy voice on laugh tracks. Once I picked it up I couldn't stop listening for it. It distressed me and made me even clumsier. Every time I slipped or fell down she shrieked higher and louder, and then there came a time when she didn't stop between falls but kept on shrieking in a breathless, broken voice that had no trace of laughter. I wasn't the only one to notice. The gym grew quiet. Eventually hers was the only voice to be heard. She didn't stop. Our coach called time-out, and we went to the sidelines to towel off and slake our thirst. People were turning in their seats to look up at her. She was standing in the top row of the bleachers, a woman I'd never seen before, a huge broad-shouldered woman wearing curlers and tore-ador pants. She had her hands over her face. Her shoulders

jerked as muffled barking sounds escaped her. A short man
with scarlet cheeks and downcast eyes was leading her by the
elbow. They passed along their row and down the steps, then
across the gym floor to the exit, the woman barking convul-
sively through her fingers.

The game resumed, but with a difference. The crowd
was quieter now, almost hushed. When the other team had
the ball, a few scattered voices called polite encouragement;
when they made a basket the applause was subdued. The
room came into focus for me. I caught my breath, found my
rhythm, and settled into the game. I still had trouble keeping
my feet, but nobody laughed when I fell down. The crowd
was on my side now, and the other team seemed to know
it. They played with an air of deference, almost of apology. I
began to see myself from the stands and became sentimentally
aroused by the consciousness of my own nobility and grit in
seeing this game through. I had wrenched my knee slightly
in a fall, and I parlayed this annoyance into a limp sufficiently
pronounced to draw sympathy without forcing the referee to
end the game. I hobbled gamely up and down the floor and
the other team slowed down too, as if to refuse any further
advantage over us.

They won by a mile. When the buzzer went off, their
coach ran onto the court and had them give us three cheers.

NORMA AND BOBBY were late picking me up. The parking lot
was almost empty when they pulled in.

"Who won?" Norma asked. She pushed the door open for me and leaned forward as I squeezed past her into the backseat.

"They did."

"Next time," Bobby said.

Norma closed the door and slid back over next to Bobby. They looked at each other. He put the car in gear and drove slowly out of the lot. It was warm inside the car, cloying. Norma stretched, fiddled with the radio, teased the hair on Bobby's neck. She called him Bobo, her pet name for him, and said something that made him laugh. Her voice was low, her movements languorous. I watched them. As we drove on I kept watching them. I was nervously alert, suspicious without knowing what I was suspicious of. And then I knew. The knowledge did not come to me as a thought but as a sudden physical oppression. I had never understood before, not really, what they did when they were off alone together. I knew they fooled around but I thought they were mainly friends. I never thought she would do this to me.

In the darkness of the backseat I sat rigid and mute, punching her, slapping her, calling her names. I took away the blue convertible I was going to give her, the furs and filmy clothes. I threw her out of the mansion.

Then I let her back in. There was no choice. And later, whenever I heard Ray Charles sing "I Can't Stop Lovin' You," I just had to stop and get sad for a while.

W hen my mother joined the rifle club she recruited several other wives, and more couples signed up as time went on. It had been a loose society of beery guys who liked to plink at cans, but that changed. Some of the new members were serious shooters, and after the club got smeared by a couple of other clubs the old members either got serious themselves or dropped out.

My mother did well at matches. She loved to win. Winning made her jaunty and bright. Her shooting jacket was covered with badges and ribbons, but Dwight's jacket had none, because he always lost. He claimed that the Remington target rifle he'd bought was imperfectly balanced. He bought another, and when that also proved defective he bought a third. He continued to lose, but it wasn't from lack of trying. He spent two or three nights a week practicing at the club, and used the long hallway in our house as a dry-firing range. He fixed a target to the door at one end and sighted down at it from the other, arms twined through the straps, cheek mashed to the stock. Breathe in, breathe out, squeeze off. Breathe in, breathe out, squeeze off. When I came in from my paper route I often found myself looking down the barrel of Dwight's latest piece, which he, in outrageous violation of the code governing even unloaded weapons, held on me until I moved out of the way.

Dwight made Pearl and me come along when the club had matches in other towns. They always turned out the same: my mother did well and Dwight choked. He pretended not to care, but on the drive home he began to sulk. His face darkened, his lower lip protruded, his neck sank down into his shoulders. Pearl and I kept quiet in the backseat until one of us forgot and started humming, or said something. Then Dwight snarled so viciously that my mother felt obliged to put in a soothing word. He turned on her and said that as far as he knew he was still the father of this so-called family, or did she have another candidate?

"Dwight . . ." she said.

"Dwight," he mimicked, not sounding at all like her.

Then, until we reached Marblemount, he railed at her for refusing to appreciate his sacrifice in taking on a divorced woman with a kid, let alone a kid like me, a liar, a thief, a sissy. If my mother argued back he accused her of being disloyal; if she did not argue he became apoplectic with the sound of his own voice. Nothing could stop him but the sight of the Marblemount tavern.

He pulled into the parking lot and jammed on the brakes, skidding through the loose gravel. He got out, stuck his head back inside, pronounced some final judgment on us and slammed the door. My mother sat with Pearl and me for a while, stony-faced, watching the tavern. She never cried. Finally she got out of the car and went inside herself.

*   *   *

I WAS A liar. Even though I lived in a place where everyone knew who I was, I couldn't help but try to introduce new versions of myself as my interests changed, and as other versions failed to persuade. I was also a thief. Dwight's reason for calling me one was trivial, based on my having taken his hunting knife without permission. My thefts were real. I'd begun by stealing candy from the rooms of newspaper subscribers who lived in the bachelors' quarters. Most of these men kept candy around. I fell into the habit of taking a piece here, a piece there. Then I stole money from them. At first I took only small change, to buy Cokes and ice cream, but later I stole fifty-cent pieces and even dollar bills. I stashed the money in an ammunition box under one of the barracks.

My idea was to steal enough to run away. I was ready to do anything to get clear of Dwight. I even thought of killing him, shooting him down some night while he was picking on my mother. I not only carried newspapers, I read them, and reading them had taught me that you can kill a man and get away with it. You just had to appear in the right role, like Cheryl Crane when she stabbed Johnny Stampanato to death for threatening Lana Turner.

Sometimes I took the Winchester down when I heard Dwight start in on my mother, but his abuse was more boring than dangerous. She didn't respect him. She looked down on him. He was doing just fine until we came along. Who did she think she was? Mainly I wanted to shoot him just to quiet him down.

Dwight wasn't wrong when he called me a liar and a thief, but these accusations did not hurt me, because I did not see myself that way. Only one of his charges had stinging power—that I was a sissy. My best friend was a thoroughbred sissy, and because of our friendship I worried that others might think the same of me. To put myself in the clear I habitually mocked Arthur, always behind his back, imitating his speech and way of walking, even betraying his secrets. I also got into fights. I didn't fight Arthur again, but I had learned from him the trick of going crazy when insulted. I had also learned that getting hit a few times wouldn't kill me and that other people, even Dwight, would treat me with a certain deference for a few days after a fight. And of course it made other boys think twice about their words, to know that they were accountable for them.

All of Dwight's complaints against me had the aim of giving me a definition of myself. They succeeded, but not in the way he wished. I defined myself by opposition to him. In the past I had been ready, even when innocent, to believe any evil thing of myself. Now that I had grounds for guilt I could no longer feel it.

WHILE PEARL AND I waited in the car we did our best to get on each other's nerves. Pearl hummed. Her humming had nothing to do with music. It held to no pattern of melody or rhythm but spun itself out endlessly, moronic as me cracking my knuckles, which was what I did to get her goat. Crack. Crack. Crack. Crack. Crack.

We could keep this up for quite a while. Once it got boring I went for walks along the road, just far enough away that I could still see the tavern but Pearl couldn't see me and would, I hoped, imagine herself abandoned, and become afraid. I stood on the roadside with my collar up and my hands in my pockets, watching the lights of passing cars. I was a murderer on the run, a drifter about to be swept up into the passion of a lonely woman . . .

When I got tired of this I went back to the car. By now I would be lonely myself, dying to talk, but our official position was that we couldn't stand each other. Pearl and I sat in our corners and stared out our windows until I couldn't take another second of it; then I leaned over the seat and turned the radio on. Pearl warned me not to, but she didn't really mean it. She wanted to listen to the radio as much as I did. We were both big fans of *American Bandstand* and the local product, *Seattle Bandstand*. She watched them at home. I watched them at the houses of kids along my route, staying for the length of a song and then tearing down the street to my next outpost, hooking papers over my head as I ran.

I knew all the words to all the songs. So did Pearl. And as we sat in the darkness with music flooding the car we could not stop ourselves from singing along, at first privately, then together. Pearl didn't have a good voice but I never ragged her about it. That would have been too low, like ragging her about her bald spot. Anyway, you didn't need a good voice for the songs we liked; you needed timing and inflection. Pearl had these, and she could do backup and harmony. You can't sing harmony without leaning close together, taking cues from a nod, a sudden narrowing of the eyes, an intake of breath, and when it's going well you have to smile. There's no way not to smile. We did some songs well—"To Know Him Is to Love Him," "My Happiness," "Mister Blue," most of the Everly Brothers—and we sang them as if to each other, smiling, face to face.

Until Dwight came out of the tavern. Then we turned off the radio and leaned back into our corners. Dwight walked toward the car with my mother following a few steps behind, her arms crossed, her eyes on the ground. She didn't look like a winner now. Dwight got in smelling of bourbon. My mother stayed outside. She said she wouldn't get in unless Dwight gave her the keys. He just sat there, and after a time she got in. As he pulled the car out of the lot my mother gnawed at her lower lip and watched the road come at us.

"Please, Dwight," she said.

"Please, Dwight," he mimicked.

As we went into the first curve I felt Pearl's fingers sinking into my forearm.

"Please, Dwight," I said.

"*Please, Dwight,*" he said.

And then he took us through the turns above the river, tires wailing, headlights swinging between cliff and space, and the more we begged him the faster he went, only slowing down for a breath after the really close calls, and then laughing to show he wasn't afraid.

When I was alone in the house I went through everyone's private things. One day I found in my mother's bureau a letter from her brother Stephen, who lived in Paris. It was filled with descriptions of the city and the pleasures to be had there. I read it a couple of times, then copied the address from the flimsy blue envelope and put it back in the drawer.

That night I wrote my uncle a long letter in which I created a nightmare picture of our life in Chinook. It seemed true enough as I wrote it, but I got carried away. At the end of the letter I pleaded with my uncle to bring my mother and me to Paris. If he would just help us get started, I said, we'd be on our feet in no time. We would find jobs and pay him back whatever we owed. I said I didn't know how much longer we could hold out—everything depended on him. I plastered an envelope with stamps and mailed it off.

I waited a few days for his answer, then forgot about it.

MY MOTHER CAUGHT me on the steps one afternoon as I was coming in from my paper route. She said she wanted me to take a walk with her. Not far from the house there was a

153

footbridge over the river, and when we got there she stopped and asked me what in the world I had written to her brother.

I said I didn't remember, exactly.

"It must've been pretty bad," she said. When I didn't answer, she asked, "How did you get his address?"

I told her I'd found the letter on top of her bureau. She shook her head and looked out over the water. "I was just trying to help," I said.

"Read this," she said, and handed me a blue envelope. Inside was another letter from Uncle Stephen. He expressed his shock and sympathy at the wretchedness of our condition, but explained that he wasn't able to launch a rescue operation on the scale of the one I had proposed. They didn't have room for both of us, and as far as finding jobs was concerned we had no prospects at all. We didn't speak French, and even if we did we would never be able to get working papers. I belonged in school, anyway. The whole idea was ridiculous.

Still, he and his wife wanted to do what they could. They had talked it over and come up with a plan they wanted us to consider. This was that I should come alone to Paris and live with them and go to school with my cousins, one of whom, Kathy, was my age and would be able to help me make friends and learn the ropes. While I lived with them my mother would be free to get away from Dwight and look for work. Once she got settled, really settled—say in a year or so—I could rejoin her.

My uncle referred to a check he'd apparently enclosed, saying he was sorry he couldn't send more. He hoped my mother would give every consideration to his plan, which seemed to him a good one. In the future he thought it would be best if she wrote him herself.

"What do you think?" my mother asked.

"I don't know," I said. "Paris."

She said, "Just think of it. You in Paris."

"Paris," I said.

She nodded. "So what do you think?"

"I don't know. What about you?"

"He has some pretty good points. It would be a great experience for you, living in Paris. And it would give me some time to see how things go here."

I was trying to be sober and so was she, but we ended up grinning at each other.

"Just don't say anything about the check," my mother said.

DWIGHT WAS ALL for packing me off to Paris. The thought that I would soon be leaving softened him and disposed him toward reminiscence. He said that his travels during the war had given him a whole nother outlook on life. He gave me advice on how to treat Frenchmen, and counseled me to be broad-minded when confronted with their effeminate customs. I heard a lot about the French people's appetite for frogs, and learned that this was how they came to be known as Frogs by the people of other nations. From a set of pre-World War I English encyclopedias he had bought at a yard sale, Dwight read me long passages on French history (tumultuous, despotic, distinguished by the Gallic taste for conspiracy and betrayal), French culture (full of Gallic wit and high spirits, but generally derivative, superficial, arid, and atheistic), and the French national character (endowed with a certain Gallic warmth and charm, but excitable, sensual, and, on the whole, unreliable).

Pearl burned. She could not accept that I was going to live in Paris. I added to her unhappiness by treating her with condescension. I also condescended to Arthur and my other friends, as if they had served their purpose and were already dematerializing into quaint, vaporous memories. At school I asked for and received permission to take time off from my regular studies to complete a series of "special projects" on the history, culture, and national character of France.

All my impressions of Paris came from American movies, in which everyone wore berets and striped jerseys and sat around smoking cigarettes while accordian music played in the background. It was the same instrument I heard in the background of my mother's Piaf records. But I didn't know that it was an accordian. I thought it was a harmonica, and that everyone in Paris knew how to play one. So I bought a harmonica, a Hohner Marine Band, and wandered around Chinook blowing on it, honking out moony approximations of "La Vie en Rose" and the theme from *Moulin Rouge* to prepare myself for my new life in Paris, France.

* * *

I WAS SUPPOSED to leave as soon as I finished seventh grade so I'd have the summer to study French and learn my way around before starting school in the fall. My mother had made reservations for me on planes from Seattle to New York, and New York to Paris. She was about to drive me down to Mount Vernon to apply for a passport when my uncle changed the plan.

He wrote that he and his wife had had second thoughts about the original idea. It simply didn't make sense for us to go to the immense trouble and cost of uprooting me from my family, my community, and my school, not to mention my language, only to do it all over again a year later. It took more than a year to get to know a country as complex as France. And there was also the question of authority. They gathered that I had a history of discipline problems. How could they be sure that I would obey them when I didn't seem to obey my own mother, especially since I knew I'd be leaving at the end of the year?

They foresaw a lot of problems, to say the least.

But they still wanted to help, and believed I would benefit greatly from the experience of foreign travel, a good school, and a well-regulated family. So they proposed that I should live with them not for just one year but for five years, until I finished high school. And to make sure that I regarded them as my own family, they offered to become my own family. They offered to adopt me. In fact they insisted on adopting me as a condition of the rest of the plan. This was, they said, the only way it could work. My mother was welcome to visit whenever she wanted, of course, but they meant the adoption to be genuine and not just a *pro forma* arrangement. Henceforth I would be their son.

They knew this gave us a lot to think about. They didn't want to pressure us or hurry us in any way, but we should remember that they needed time to prepare for my arrival, and that summer was coming up fast.

I asked my mother why she'd told them I had discipline problems.

"Because it's true. It wouldn't have been fair to send you over there without telling them that."

"Thanks a lot. I guess that's it for Paris."

"Not necessarily."

"Oh, great. All I have to do is let them adopt me."

She told me to think about it. They were being very generous, she said. They were offering to share everything they had with me—even their name.

"Their name? I'd have to change my name?"

"It's a good name. It used to be mine."

When I asked my mother what she wanted, she wouldn't tell me. She said it was my decision. Though she didn't often make use of it, she had a way of going blank, impervious to scrutiny. She gave nothing away. I couldn't stare her down, or wheedle my way in, or flush her from cover by haughtily pretending that I already knew what she wasn't telling me.

But Dwight had plenty to say. The prospect of losing me not only for a year but, practically speaking, for good, brought him to a frenzy of coaxing and bullying and opinion-dispensing.

He said I would never forgive myself if I passed up a chance like this. So what if they wanted me to call them Mom and Dad. He'd call them Jesus and Mary if it meant a chance to live in Paris. Was I afraid to leave my mother? Okay, he'd fly her to Paris every summer, I had his guarantee on it, word of honor. So what was the problem? I'd better think fast, he told me, and I'd better come up with the right answer.

WHENEVER I WAS told to think about something, my mind became a desert. But this time I had no need of thought, because the answer was already there. I was my mother's son. I could not be anyone else's. When I was younger and having trouble learning to write, she sat me down at the kitchen table and covered my hand with hers and moved it through the alphabet for several nights running, and then through words and sentences until the motions assumed their own life, partly hers and partly mine. I could not, cannot, put pen to paper without having her with me. Nor swim, nor sing. I could imagine leaving her. I knew I would, someday. But to call someone else my mother was impossible. I didn't reason any of this out. It was there as instinct. I felt lesser instincts at work on me too, such as alarm at my uncle's description of his family as "well-regulated." I didn't like the sound of that at all.

And even if my mother wouldn't tell me what she wanted, or give any hints, I was sure that she wanted me to stay with her. I took her inscrutability as a concealment of this wish. Later she agreed that this was so, but maybe it wasn't all that simple at the time. She still hoped this marriage would work, was ready to put up with almost anything to make it work. The idea of another failure was abhorrent to her. But she may also have dreamed of flight and freedom—unencumbered, solitary freedom, freedom even from me. Like anyone else, she must have wanted different things at the same time. The human heart is a dark forest.

After a week or so I announced at dinner that I had decided not to go to Paris.

"The hell you aren't," Dwight said. "You're going."

"He gets to choose," Pearl said, on my side for once. "Doesn't he, Rosemary?"

My mother nodded. "That was the deal."

"The books aren't closed on this one," Dwight said. "Not yet they aren't." He looked at me. "Why do you think you aren't going?"

"I don't want to change my name."

"You don't want to change your name?"

"No sir."

He put his fork down. His nostrils were flaring. "Why not?"

"I don't know. I just don't."

"Well that's a lot of crap, because you've already changed your name once. Right?"

"Yes sir."

"Then you might as well change the other name too, make a clean sweep."

"But it's my last name."

"Oh, for Christ's sake. You think anybody cares what you call yourself?"

I shrugged.

"Don't badger him," my mother said. "He's already made up his mind."

"We're talking about Paris!" Dwight shouted.

"It was his choice," she said.

Dwight jabbed his finger at me. "You're going."

"Only if he wants to," my mother said.

"You're going," he repeated.

EXCEPT FOR ARTHUR, people didn't say much about my not going to Paris. They'd probably thought all along that it was just one of my stories. Arthur called me Frenchy for a while, then lost interest as I seemed to lose interest, while in secret I went on thinking of cobbled streets and green roofs, and cafés where fast, smoky-voiced women sang songs about their absolute lack of remorse.

D wight said that he had once seen Lawrence Welk in the dining car of a train. Dwight said that he'd walked right up to him and told him that he was his favorite conductor, and he probably did, for it was true that he loved the champagne music of Lawrence Welk better than any other music. Dwight had a large collection of Lawrence Welk records. When the Lawrence Welk show came on TV we were expected to watch it with him, and be quiet, and get up only during commercials. Dwight pulled his chair up close to the set. He leaned forward as the bubbles rose over the Champagne Orchestra and Lawrence Welk came onstage salaaming in every direction, crying out declarations of humility in his unctuous, brain-scalding Swedish kazoo of a voice.

Dwight's eyes widened at the virtuosity of Big Tiny Little Junior, who played ragtime piano while looking over his shoulder at the camera. He gazed with chaste ardor at the Lovely Champagne Lady Alice Lon, who smiled the same tremulous smile through every note of every song until she got canned and replaced by the Lovely Champagne Lady Norma Zimmer. He gloated over the Lovely Little Lennon Sisters as if they were his own daughters, and laughed out loud at the cruel jokes Lawrence Welk made at the expense of his slobbering

Irish tenor, Joe Feeney. Joe Feeney was the latest addition to the Champagne Ensemble and obviously felt himself on pretty shaky ground, especially after the Lovely Champagne Lady Alice Lon was sent packing and then the Ragtime Piano Virtuoso Big Tiny Little Junior got replaced by the Ragtime Piano Virtuoso Jo Ann Castle, who pummeled the keys like a butcher tenderizing meat. When Joe Feeney sang he held nothing back. He worked himself up to the point of tears, and flecks of saliva flew off his wet lips. You had the feeling that Joe Feeney was singing for his life.

About halfway through the show, Dwight would take out his old Conn saxophone and finger the stops in time to the music. Sometimes, when he got really carried away, he would forget himself and blow on it, and a squawk would come out.

AFTER NORMA GRADUATED from Concrete High she moved down to Seattle. She worked in an office where she met a man named Kenneth who took her for long drives in his Austin Healey sports car and tried to talk her into getting married. Norma called my mother all the time and asked for advice. What should she do? She still loved Bobby Crow, but Bobby wasn't going anywhere. He didn't even have a job. Kenneth was ambitious. On the other hand, nobody liked him. He had very strong opinions about everything and was also a Seventh-day Adventist. But that wasn't it, exactly. Kenneth just didn't have a very good personality.

Then Norma called up and said she'd decided to marry Kenneth. She refused to explain her decision, but insisted it was final. Naturally, she wanted to invite Kenneth to Chinook to meet the family, and it was finally settled that he should come up during Christmas, when Skipper would also be home.

Dwight got the spirit that year. He made a wreath for the door and hung pine boughs all over the living room. A couple of weeks before Christmas he and I drove up into the mountains to get a tree. It was early afternoon, a cold light rain falling. Dwight drank from a pint bottle as we scouted the woods. We found a fine blue spruce growing all by itself in the middle of a clearing, and Dwight let me cut it down while he took nips off his bottle and squinted up at the misty peaks all around us. Once I got the tree down we started wrestling it through the dense growth, back toward the fire road where we'd left the car. We had walked a good distance and the going was rough. I could hear Dwight laboring for breath and muttering when he stumbled. I kept waiting for him to bark at me, but he never did. He was that pleased about Norma coming home.

After dinner that night Dwight went into the living room with a can of spray paint and began to shake it. He was very thorough when it came to painting, and if he was using spray paint he always followed the directions to the letter and shook the can well. The agitator rattled loudly as he swung the can back and forth. Pearl and I were doing our homework at the dining-room table. We pretended not to watch. My mother was out somewhere or else she would've asked him what he thought he was doing, and possibly even stopped him.

When he finished shaking the can, Dwight pulled the tree into the middle of the living room and walked around it two or three times. Then, starting at the top and working his way down, he proceeded to spray it with white paint. I thought he meant to put a few splashes here and there to suggest snow, but he sprayed the whole thing—trunk and all. The needles drank up the paint and turned faintly blue again. Dwight put on another coat. It took him three cans before he was done, but the tree stayed white.

By the next day, when we decorated the tree, the needles had already begun to drop off. Every time you touched a limb it set off a little cascade of them. No one said anything. My mother hung a few balls, then sat down and stared at the tree.

The needles kept falling, pattering softly down on the white crepe paper spread around the trunk. By the time Norma and Skipper arrived the tree was half bare. They had driven up together from Seattle; Kenneth had to work, but he was all set to join us the following day.

Norma must have told Bobby Crow she was coming. He showed up just after dinner that night, restless and grim, silent when Skipper tried to banter with him. He took Norma somewhere, then drove her back a couple of hours later. But she didn't get out of the car. The rest of us sat around in the living room, and watched the lights blink on the tree, and talked about anything but the fact that Norma was still outside with Bobby Crow. The lights didn't blink at different times like twinkling stars but all at once, flashing on and off like a neon sign outside a roadhouse.

I was in bed when Norma finally came inside and ran to her room, giving long ululating cries that appalled me and made me cringe in anticipation. I heard Pearl try to soothe her, then my mother joined them and I heard her voice too, lower than Pearl's, the two of them speaking sometimes in turn and sometimes together so that their voices formed one murmurous braid of sound. Skipper shifted in his bed but slept on, and in time, as Norma's keening subsided, I lay back and went to sleep myself.

KENNETH PULLED UP the next afternoon and by dinnertime we all hated him. He knew it, and relished it, even sought it out. As soon as he stepped out of his Austin Healey, he started complaining about the remoteness of the camp and the discomfort of the drive and the imprecision of the directions Norma had left behind for him. He had a fussy, aggrieved voice and thin, disappointed lips. He wore a golf cap and perforated leather gloves that snapped across the wrist. He removed one of his gloves as he complained, tugging delicately at each finger, then going on to the next until the glove came free. He took off the other just as slowly and carefully, then turned to Norma. "Don't I get a kiss?"

She bent forward to peck him on the cheek but he seized her face between his hands and kissed her long and full on the lips. It was obvious that he was French-kissing her. We stood watching this and smiling the same foolish smiles we had brought outside to welcome him with.

After Kenneth had wolfed down a sandwich, Dwight made the mistake of offering him a drink. "Oh, boy," Kenneth said. "I guess you don't know much about me." He said that he believed he had a duty to lay his cards on the table, and so he did.

"I don't know," Dwight said. "I don't see the harm in a drink now and then."

"I'm sure you don't," Kenneth said. "I'm sure the drug fiend doesn't see the harm in a needle now and then."

This led to an exchange of words. My mother stepped in and acted jolly and moved us from the kitchen into the living room, where she must have hoped that the presence of the tree and the gifts would remind us why we were together, and call us to our better selves. But Kenneth started laying more cards on the table. There truly was no end of them. Skipper finally said, "Look, Kenneth . . . why don't you lay off?"

"What are you afraid of, Skipper?"

"Afraid?" Skipper's eyelids fluttered as if he were trying to confirm some improbable image.

"I only tell you this because I love you," Kenneth said, "but you are very frightened people. Very frightened. But hey, there's no need to be—the news is good!"

"Just who the hell do you think you are?" Dwight said.

Kenneth smiled. "Go on. I can take it."

Norma tried to change the subject but Kenneth could take any comment and find something in it to deplore. Argument was the only kind of sound he knew how to make. And if you didn't give in to him he smirked and offered you his pity for being so ignorant and misled. He wasn't reluctant to get personal. Soon enough Dwight and Skipper got personal back, and then Pearl and I put our oars in. Insulting this man was a profound pleasure, and a pleasure not only for us; a flush of excitement came into his pallid face as the words got meaner and harder to take back. He kept our blood up by saying, "If you think that bothers me, you're sadly mistaken," and "Sorry, try again," and "I've had worse than that."

This went on for some time. As we baited him Kenneth smiled in a secretive way and sucked on an empty Yellow-Bole pipe with which, he later told me, he strengthened his will power by tempting himself to smoke.

Norma was mute. She sat next to Kenneth on the sofa and stared at the floor while he absently rubbed his hand up and down her back. Every time he touched her I felt despair. At last my mother came in from the kitchen and suggested that Norma take Kenneth out and show him around Chinook. Norma nodded and stood up, but Kenneth said he didn't want to leave now, just when things were getting interesting.

Norma implored him with her eyes.

Finally he left with her. In the wake of his going we exchanged looks of exultation and shame. A fidgety silence came upon us. One by one we drifted away to other parts of the house.

But at dinner it started up again. Kenneth couldn't stop himself. Even when he was quiet you could feel him preparing his next charge. The only thing that could shut him up was the TV. When the TV came on Kenneth went silent, staring and still as an owl in a tree.

Over the next couple of days my mother talked each of us into spending some time alone with him so we could get to know one another as individuals. This proved a mistake. Some people are better left unknown. Our walks and drives with Kenneth ended early and culminated in shouts and slamming doors. Years later my mother told me he'd made a pass at her.

WE COULD ALL see that Norma didn't love Kenneth. But she stayed next to him, and submitted to his demonstrations of passion, and refused to say a word against him. She even, in the end, married him. But not before Dwight had nearly killed himself trying to stop her. He drove down to Seattle almost every weekend, sometimes bringing us along, more often by himself, always with some new scheme for luring her away from Kenneth. Nothing worked. He returned late Sunday night or early Monday morning, eyes bloodshot from the long drive, too tired and baffled even to quarrel.

Norma married Kenneth, and had their baby, and they moved into a duplex near Bothell. When we came down for visits she acted happy and never complained about anything. But she was pale and angular, all her lazy lushness gone. Her green eyes blazed in the starkness of her face. She had taken up smoking—out on their little patio where Kenneth wouldn't smell it when he got home—and she continuously excused herself during our visits to go outside and puff greedily on a cigarette, tapping her feet and looking up at the sky, now and then glancing back at us through the sliding glass door.

I saw Bobby Crow in Concrete a year or so later, just after I'd started high school there. He was standing beside a truck with some other men, most of them Indians. Bobby still had a measure of renown for his gridiron magic, and I thought I would impress the two boys I was with by a show of familiarity. As we walked past the truck I said, "Hey, Bobo, how's it going?" The men fell quiet and looked over at us. Bobby fixed me with a stare. "Who the hell are you talking to?" he said. His eyes were full of murder.

WE WATCHED TV most of Christmas Eve. When it got dark, Dwight left the house lights off so we could get the full effect of the lights on the tree. We broke to eat, then went back to the set. By the time the "Lawrence Welk Christmas Special" came on we were glassy-eyed and slack-jawed, stunned with viewing. The Champagne Orchestra played a medley of Christmas favorites, the sacred and profane mixed effervescently together, and then someone wearing knee-britches and a tricorner hat acted the part of Franz Gruber while Lawrence Welk intoned the narrative: "It was Christmas Eve in the little town of Oberndorf, and snow was falling as the organist Franz Gruber made his weary way to the little church that was soon to become famous throughout the world. . . ." The Gruber character paused on the church steps, looked up suddenly with the fire of inspiration in his eyes, then dashed inside and plunked out "Silent Night." He had to change a couple of notes here and there, but after he got it right the orchestra segued in and subsumed it into their own champagne arrangement, with Joe Feeney sobbing out a verse a cappella at the very end.

The scene shifted. We found ourselves in an elegant room where, under a shimmering tree, The Lovely Little Lennon Sisters began to sing a medley of their own. Firelight gleamed on their faces. Snow fell slowly past the window behind them, a glockenspiel chimed in accompaniment. They were singing "Chestnuts Roasting on an Open Fire" when Dwight nudged me and motioned me to follow him. He looked pleased with himself. "It's about time we got some use out of those chestnuts," he said.

The chestnuts. Almost two years had passed since I'd shucked them and stored them away. In all that time no one had said a word about them. They'd been forgotten by everyone but me, and I'd kept my mouth shut because I didn't want to remind Dwight to give me the job again.

We climbed up into the attic and worked our way down to where I'd put the boxes. It was cramped and musty. From below I could hear faint voices singing. Dwight led the way, probing the darkness with a flashlight. When he found the boxes he stopped and held the beam on them. Mold covered the cardboard sides and rose from the tops of the boxes like dough swelling out of a breadpan. Its surface, dark and solid-looking, gullied and creased like cauliflower, glistened in the light. Dwight played the beam over the boxes, then turned it on the basin where the beaver, also forgotten these two years past, had been left to cure. Only a pulp remained. This too was covered with mold, but a different kind than the one that had gotten the chestnuts. This mold was white and transparent, a network of gossamer filaments that had flowered to a height of two feet or so above the basin. It was like cotton candy but more loosely spun. And as Dwight played the light over it I saw something strange. The mold had no features, of course, but its outline somehow suggested the shape of the beaver it had consumed: a vague cloud-picture of a beaver crouching in the air.

If Dwight noticed it he didn't say anything. I followed him back downstairs and into the living room. My mother had gone to bed, but everyone else was still watching TV. Dwight picked up his saxaphone again and played silently along with the Champagne Orchestra. The tree blinked. Our faces darkened and flared, darkened and flared.

By the time I started my first year at Concrete High School, I had over eighty dollars squirreled away in the ammunition box. Some of it had been given to me by customers on my paper route, as tips for good service; the rest I'd stolen from other customers. Eighty dollars seemed a lot of money, more than enough for my purpose, which was to run away to Alaska.

I planned to travel alone under an assumed name. Later on, when I had my feet on the ground, I would send for my mother. It was not hard to imagine our reunion in my cabin: her grateful tears and cries of admiration at the pelt-covered walls, the racks of guns, the tame wolves dozing before the fire.

Our Scout troop went to Seattle every November for The Gathering of the Tribes. In the morning we competed with other troops. In the afternoon all the Scouts converged on Glenvale, an amusement park reserved that day for our use. Dwight always went drinking with some other Scoutmasters, then picked me up outside Glenvale for the drive home. This year he would have a long wait. He would have a long wait, and a long drive home alone, and a long explanation to make to my mother when he pulled up to the house without me.

I told no one but Arthur, who kept my secrets even when I betrayed his. He liked the plan. He thought so highly of it that he asked to be included. At first I said no. Being on my own was the whole idea. And Arthur had no money. But a few days before The Gathering of the Tribes I told him I'd changed my mind, that he could come along after all. I gave Arthur this news with a show of reluctance, as if I were doing him a favor, but really I was just afraid to be alone.

ARTHUR'S FATHER, CAL, worked on the turbines in the power-house. He thought I was a great wit because I could always tell him a new joke. I got the jokes from "Today's Chuckle," a filler they ran on the front page of the paper. Whenever I visited Arthur, Cal said, "Well, Jackaroony, what's the word?"

"Woman bought three hundred pounds of steel wool. Says she's going to knit a stove."

"Knit a stove! Knit a stove, you say! Oh that's rich, that's a beauty . . ." and Cal would hold his sides and reel back and forth while Arthur and Mrs. Gayle looked on with disgust.

He was a simple, sunny man, well-liked in the camp. Even the kids called him Cal. I never heard anyone call him Mr. Gayle. Once, at a beach house belonging to friends of theirs, I persuaded Cal to let me take Arthur out for a spin in a sailboat, claiming that back in Florida I had pretty much lived with a tiller in my hand. After being very nearly swept out to sea we ran aground a mile from the house. Arthur went up the beach and got Cal, but Cal didn't know how to sail either, so he had to pull the boat home through the surf. He had a hard time of it—the wind was stiff and the waves high—but he didn't stop laughing the whole way back.

Arthur and Mrs. Gayle were complicated. They were complicated by themselves and exotically complicated when together, playing off each other in long cryptic riffs like a pair of scat singers, then falling heavily, portentously silent. They had a way of turning silence into accusation. Cal could not begin to understand them. Under their scrutiny he smiled and blinked his eyes. This seemed to compound the unspoken charges against him.

Mrs. Gayle was a snob. She and Cal had been among the first to move into the camp, and she would have nothing to do with those who came afterwards. Mrs. Gayle carried herself as one betrayed into an inferior version of life. The articles of this betrayal remained unpublished, but it was understood that Cal was to blame; also, to some degree, Arthur. Mrs. Gayle was disappointed. Every couple of weeks she dulled her disappointment by shopping in Mount Vernon with Liz Dempsey, a friend of hers from another Founding Family. They got all dressed up and had boozy lunches and bought things. Mostly they bought useless little things Mrs. Gayle called notions, but sometimes they concluded more serious purchases. I was in the house one night when Mrs. Gayle came back with an expensive lamp that had at its base a rickshaw pulled by a grinning coolie whose legs churned furiously when you pressed down on his hat.

The two women took Arthur and me along on a couple of their sprees. I enjoyed listening to Mrs. Gayle talk about other people in the camp, impaling them with a word or phrase so uncanny I could never see them afterward without remembering it. She knew that I admired her tongue. She liked me for that, and for the fact that my brother Geoffrey was a student at Princeton. She said the words *Ivy League* often, and tenderly. I was a big snob myself, so we got along fine.

Arthur's disappointment was more combative. He refused to accept as final the proposition that Cal and Mrs. Gayle were his real parents. He told me, and I contrived to believe, that he was adopted, and that his real family was descended from Scottish liege men who had followed Bonnie Prince Charlie into exile in France. I read the same novels Arthur read, but managed not to notice the correspondences between their plots and his. And Arthur in turn did not question the stories I told him. I told him that my family was descended from Prussian aristocrats—"Junkers," I said, pronouncing the word with pedantic accuracy—whose estates had been seized after the war. I got the idea for this narrative from a book called *The Prussians*. It was full of pictures of Crusaders, kings, castles, splendid hussars riding to the attack at Waterloo, cold-eyed Von Richthofen standing beside his triplane.

Arthur was a great storyteller. He talked himself into reveries where every word rang with truth. He repeated ancient conversations. He rendered the creak of oars in their oarlocks. He spoke in the honest brogue of the crofter, the despicable whine of the traitor. In Arthur's voice the mist rose above the loch and the pipes skirled; bold deeds were done, high words of troth plighted, and I believed them all.

I was his perfect witness and he was mine. We listened without objection to stories of usurped nobility that grew in preposterous intricacy with every telling. But we did not feel as if anything we said was a lie. We both believed that the real lie was told by our present unworthy circumstances.

Looking always backward, we became mired in nostalgia. We both liked old movies, which Mrs. Gayle allowed us to watch all night when I slept over, and whose fatuous obsession with aristocracy fed our own. We preferred old cars to new ones. We used antique slang. Arthur played the piano pretty well, and when we were alone in his house we sang old songs together, our voices quavering with loss:

> I wandered today to the hill, Maggie,
> To watch the scene below . . .
> The creek and the old rusty mill, Maggie,
> Where we sat in the long long ago

One night he kissed me, or I kissed him, or we kissed each other. It surprised us both. After that, whenever we felt particularly close we turned on each other. Arthur was an easy target. His voice cracked. He bathed twice a day but always gave off an ammoniac hormonal smell, the smell of growth and anxiety. He played no sports and was still a Second Class Scout, a truly pitiful rank for someone his age. As long as I didn't call him a sissy I could cut him to pieces.

I was a sitting duck myself, and Arthur had a map of my nerves. With feline insouciance he could produce a word that would knock me breathless and send me stumbling blind from the house. Sometimes he set Pepper on me. Pepper would yap at my heels all the way down the street while Arthur stood at his door and urged him on, knowing that I liked the little mutt too much to defend myself.

We had these blowups often. We'd stay clear of each other for a few days, then Arthur would call up and invite me over as if nothing had happened, and I would go.

THE GATHERING OF the Tribes was held in a high school just outside Seattle. My event was the swimming meet. I carried an overnight bag with my swimming trunks and towel, and a change of clothes for Arthur and me so our uniforms wouldn't give us away when we left Glenvale later that day and began hitching our way north.

During the Gathering I kept my distance from Arthur. I didn't want to be associated with him, and not only because of what we were planning. His uniform was baggy and un-adorned, his manner supercilious. He stood at the edges of the events and made sarcastic remarks. He didn't look like a serious Scout. I did. I held Star rank. I had a new uniform and plenty of things to wear on it. Patrol leader's insignia. The Order of the Arrow. A sash with several merit badges. To look at my merit badges you would have thought I could be dropped anywhere, in any season, just as I was, and in no time improvise a shelter and kindle a fire and snare an animal for dinner. You would have thought I could navigate by the stars. Name trees. Find, in any terrain, exactly those plants that would nourish me and toss them up in a mouth-watering salad.

And I actually could have done some of those things. The details began to fade as soon as I got the badges, but I had learned a rough kind of competence and ease in the woods. It was a gift of priceless worth. But I did not guess its value then. Then I was mainly interested in covering myself with enough insignia to look sharp, which, to my way of thinking, I did.

The swimming meet was held in the morning. I got bumped after the first couple of heats. This surprised me, though it shouldn't have—I always got bumped. But I started every meet believing that I was going to win, and ended it believing that I should have won, that I was the best swimmer there. After I got bumped I spent a long time in the shower, feeling low, then took a tour of the other events.

The big sensation at this year's Gathering was the close-order drill competition. It was dominated by a troop from Ballard led by a Scoutmaster who wore a black garrison cap with silver piping and a military-looking jacket with battle ribbons. It was not a uniform I had ever seen before, or would ever see again. His troop wore their pant legs tucked into the tops of gleaming black boots. They also sported black garrison caps. Their boots clapped resoundingly as the troop marched back and forth across the asphalt yard behind the school. The

Scoutmaster shouted commands in a harsh voice, watching his troop with a fierce, imperious expression.

Our troop didn't have a drill team and neither did most of the rest. There were only five or six other teams, and each of these was clearly outclassed by the Ballard troop. They were all business, these Ballard boys—crisp, erect, poker-faced, responsive to nothing but their Scoutmaster's voice. They drew an enormous crowd. I saw Dwight across the yard, rubbing his jaw thoughtfully.

"What a bunch of dildos," Arthur said.

I ignored him.

They lost the competition, disqualified for wearing non-regulation caps and boots. The crowd booed the judges; the Ballard troop had won, hands down. Their Scoutmaster went into a rage. He cussed at the judges and threw his cap on the ground, and when the judges didn't yield he marched his team off the yard and refused to form them up again for the awards ceremony.

I saw three boys from the Ballard troop in the cafeteria later on. They looked tough in their uniforms. I joined them at their table and told them how badly I thought they'd been screwed, and they agreed, and we got to talking. Over many such Gatherings and Councils I had developed a bluff conventioneer's talent for working the floor and "establishing ties" with boys from other troops. I'd pump them for details about the places they lived as if they hailed from Greenland or Samoa. I'd give them my name and collect theirs on pieces of paper that thickened my wallet to a fistlike roundness.

I worked my magic on these boys from Ballard and pretty soon it was old home week. I told them some of my amazing stories, like the one about the escaped lunatic who'd left his hook hanging on the door handle of Bobby Crow's car, and they told me some of theirs. They were good friends with the cousin of a guy who'd lost his dick in an automobile accident. He crashed his convertible into a tree and his girlfriend was thrown high up into the branches. When the police got her down they found the guy's dong in her mouth. If I didn't believe them I could ask anyone from Ballard.

When we ran out of true stories we told jokes. The Silver Saddle. The Glass Eye and the Wooden Leg. The Chinese Milkshake. One of them asked me if I smoked.

"Do I smoke?" I said. "Is a bear Catholic? Does the Pope shit in the woods?"

"Let's go."

The four of us walked outside and sat down under some trees beside the football field. I noticed Arthur coming toward us. He stopped under the goalposts. I couldn't believe he had followed me out here. The Ballard boys noticed him too. "Who's that?" one of them asked.

"Just a guy," I said.

"From your troop?"

I nodded.

"What's his name?"

"Arthur."

"As in *King*?"

We all laughed.

181

The Ballard boy held up a package of Hit Parades. "Hey Arthur," he yelled. "Want a weed?"

Arthur shook his head. He stuck his hands in his pocket and looked away. After a while he sauntered back toward the school.

The Ballard boy passed the Hit Parades around. He took out another, smaller package and handed it to me; it was a six-pack of Trojans. I took out the one foilwrapped rubber left inside, looked at it, then put it back in the box and returned it to him. "That was full last night," he said.

We had a few cigarettes and went back to the school to catch our rides over to Glenvale, where we agreed to meet by the roller coaster. As soon as I got in the car, Dwight started talking about how sharp the Ballard drill team was and how our troop needed something like that, something that could really make it a force to contend with. He kept it up all the way to Glenvale. I got out of the car with him still talking and said I'd meet him later on. He looked at the overnight bag. "What do you need that for?" he asked.

"That's okay," I said vaguely, and walked away from the car. I expected to hear him call me back, but he didn't.

The three Ballard boys were already in line for the roller coaster. All the rides were free that day. Everything was free except the food and the games of chance. While we waited in line we compared Ballard pussy with Concrete pussy and discussed the various roller coaster fatalities of which we had personal knowledge. Arthur stood some distance away, watching me. Finally he came up and asked me when I wanted to leave.

"In a while," I said.

"I think we should go now."

"In a while."

One of the Ballard boys offered Arthur a place in line but he shook his head and turned away. He was still waiting when I got off the ride, and he waited again when the Ballard boys and I attached ourselves to another line. He waited the whole afternoon, following us from one ride to the next. He watched me stand treat at the refreshment stand, gaily peeling bills off my wad. When we headed toward the midway he followed us, and came up to me again while one of the Ballard boys was throwing darts.

"I thought we were going to Alaska," he said.

"We are."

"Yeah, but when?"

"Look, we're *going*, okay? Jeez. Just hold your horses."

I threw some darts myself. I tossed rings. I pitched baseballs at weighted milk bottles. I tried my strength. And then I stopped by the Blackout booth.

Blackout was an unfamiliar game to me, but it looked like a snap. For a quarter you got a board with several sections marked out on it and three metal disks etched with symbols. If the symbols on a disk matched up in certain ways with the symbols on a section, you could lay the disk over the section. You received points according to the configuration of the disks on the board, and the sum of these points entitled you to prizes arranged in tiers against the back of the stall: ashtrays, paperweights, Kewpie dolls, porcelain bulldogs on the lowest tier; baseball mitts, stuffed animals, lighters shaped like pistols, clock radios, stiletto knives, ID bracelets on the next; and so on up to the topmost tier, where they kept the big prizes. Portable TVs. Binoculars. Cameras. Gold pinky rings set with diamonds. Diamond necklaces on gold chains, draped casually among the other prizes. Gold watches. And, attached to each of these prizes by a ribbon, a rolled-up one-hundred-dollar bill.

The two men behind the counter saw us eyeing the prizes. Smoke and Rusty, their names were. Rusty was thin and nervous. Smoke was a fat smiling guy with gaps between his teeth. It turned out that Smoke had been a Scout himself, so for *auld lang syne* he let each of us have a free game. Rusty tried to talk him out of it, but Smoke insisted. It was just as easy as it looked. Two of the Ballard boys won paperweights, and I racked up enough points for an ID bracelet. Rusty was getting it down for me when Smoke happened to mention that if we wanted another chance he'd let us keep the points we'd already earned and apply them toward a bigger prize. The Ballard boys had no money so they took their ashtrays, but I shelled out a quarter and told Smoke to deal. This time I came close to what I needed for the clock radio. "Can I keep the points again?" I asked.

Smoke and Rusty looked at each other. "No way," Rusty said. "The boss'll kill us."

"Fuck the boss," Smoke said. "The boss ain't here."

Smoke set me up again. I thought I'd won the points I needed but Smoke said, "Too bad, Jack. Star Straddle."

"Star Straddle?"

"Right. Star Straddle. See this star here? You got one on that section too. Means you have to straddle. Straddle's minus forty. You damn near got her, though, Jack buddy."

I asked if I could try again.

Smoke leaned over the counter and peered up and down the midway. "I don't see him coming. How about it?" he said to Rusty.

"Okay, but hurry it up," Rusty said. "Our ass is grass if he catches us."

"You better do quadruplets," Smoke told me.

"Quadruplets?" I had my wallet open. Smoke plucked out a one and said, "That's the idea. You get four times as many points this way. Kinda speeds things up."

I went way over what I needed for the clock radio. I was almost up to the binoculars. Smoke whooped, but Rusty sucked in his cheeks. "You trying to give everything away?" he said.

"Can I do quadruplets again?" I asked.

Smoke said I could. He also said I could play two boards if I wanted, and the second board would have the same number of points as the one I was playing now. That would give me a chance at two big prizes instead of just one.

"Goddamnit, Smoke," Rusty said.

I was staring into my wallet. Smoke pulled out a couple of ones and dealt me six disks off the stack, three to each board. The Ballard boys pressed around to see how I'd made out. "I got it!" I yelled.

Smoke shook his head. "Almost, buddy. Moon Forfeit. Moon Forfeit should cost you fifty points but I think we can let it go at thirty. Whaddya say, Rusty?"

Rusty grumbled. Finally he said okay. At Smoke's suggestion I opened another board and upped the stakes from quadruplets to double-quadruplets.

"Watch for the boss," Smoke said.

"Get a move on," Rusty said.

"Shit," Smoke said, "Texas Sandtrap. You almost had it, Jack."

The Ballard boys cheered me on. I opened two more boards and played all five for double-quads. My score rose on Carolina Snowflakes and Wizard Wheels, then fell again on Banana Splits, Lonely Hearts, Black Diamonds. I left my wallet on the counter and Smoke took what I owed as he dealt the disks. I was just a couple of points away from winning the whole top shelf when Smoke pushed the wallet back to me. "You're a little short, Jackson."

It was empty.

I knew the Ballard boys didn't have any money. Arthur was watching me from the small crowd that had gathered around the booth, but I knew he didn't have any money either. I asked Smoke if I could have one last deal.

"Sorry, Jack. No pay, no play."

"Just one? Please?"

His eyes went past me. He smiled at the the kids watching. "You saw it happen right here," he said. "Man almost walked off with the store. You there, Carrot-top—that's right, you—don't be shy, come on up, first game's on the house. Used to be a Scout myself."

"No free games!" Rusty said. "The boss'll kill us."

"Please, Smoke," I said. Still smiling, he shuffled the disks. He didn't exactly ignore me; I wasn't even there.

"Here," Rusty said, and shoved something at me. "Take a ride or something."

It was a stuffed animal, a big pink pig with black trotters and a ring in its nose. I carried it up the midway, walking with the Ballard boys but unable to talk for the thickness in my throat. Sounds reached me from a distance. I floated without consciousness of movement. We walked here and there. At some point the Ballard boys climbed on a ride together and I lost them. I never even got their addresses.

AFTER THE PARK closed I stood by the gate with some other Scouts from my troop. Except for me, they had driven down to Seattle that morning in groups of five and six with parents who had relatives they could visit until it was time to drive home. Dwight and I had come down by ourselves.

While we waited to get picked up I tried to persuade Arthur to drive back with me and Dwight. I knew that Dwight would be drunk, and I didn't want to be alone with him. But Arthur wouldn't talk to me. As I spoke he looked away. I begged him shamelessly and at last he said, "Why should I?"

I said, "I'd do it for you."

"Hah," he said. But it was true, and he knew it. After a while he said, "Outstanding performance, Wolff. Truly outstanding."

We were among the last to go. When I saw the car coming I held the pig out to Arthur. I had not been able to think of an explanation for it. "Here," I said. "You can have it."

"What do I want that thing for?"

"Come on, take it. Please."

He said, "Well, we're being very polite tonight, aren't we?" But he took it. And that was what Dwight stared at as we walked toward him through the blaze of the headlights, this glowing pink pig carried by the sissy Arthur Gayle. And as if he knew how Dwight would describe the sight later on, Arthur, who despised him, smirked at Dwight, and wriggled and pranced every step of the way.

When I got home from Concrete one night there was a big dog sleeping on the floor of the utility room. It was an ugly dog. Its short yellow coat was bare in patches, and one ear hung in pennant-like shreds. It had a pink, almost hairless tail. As I began to walk past, the dog came awake. Its eyes were yellow. At first it just looked at me, but when I moved again it gave a low growl. I yelled for someone to come.

Dwight stuck his head through the doorway and the dog got up and started licking his hands. Dwight asked what the problem was and I told him the dog had growled at me.

Dwight said, "Good, he's supposed to. He doesn't know you yet. Champion," he said, "this is Jack. Let him smell your hands," he told me. "Go on, he won't bite."

I held my hand out and Champion sniffed it. *"Jack,"* Dwight said to him. *"Jack."*

I asked Dwight whose dog it was. He told me it was mine.

"Mine?"

"You said you wanted a dog."

"Not this one."

"Well, he's yours. You paid for him," he added.

I asked what he meant, I paid for him, but Dwight wouldn't tell me. I found out a few minutes later. Something

189

was wrong in my room. Then I saw that my Winchester was gone. I stared at the pine rack I had made for it in shop. I stared at the rack as if I'd overlooked the rifle the first time, and only needed to look more carefully to see it. I sat on my bed for a while, then I stood up and walked out to the living room, where Dwight was watching television.

I said, "My Winchester is gone."

"That dog is purebred weimaraner," Dwight said, keeping his eyes on the TV.

"I don't want it. I want my Winchester."

"Then you're shit out of luck, because your Winchester is on its way to Seattle."

"But that was *my* rifle!"

"And Champ's your dog! Jesus! I trade some old piece of crap for a valuable hunting dog and what do you do? Piss and moan, piss and moan."

"I'm not pissing and moaning."

"The hell you aren't. You can just make your own deals from now on."

My mother was at a political conference. She had done some local organizing for the Democratic party in the last state election, and now they were trying to get her to work for Adlai Stevenson. When she got home the next day I met her outside and told her about the rifle.

She nodded as if she'd already heard the story. "I knew he'd do something," she said.

They had it out after I went to bed. Dwight made some noise but she backed him down. The rifle belonged to me, she said. He could yell all he wanted but on that point there was nothing to discuss. She made Dwight agree that when Champion's owner sent up the AKC papers he'd promised to send, papers that would prove the dog's illustrious line of descent, Dwight would call him and arrange to drive Champion down to Seattle and get my rifle back. He couldn't do that now because he didn't know the man's last name or address.

In this way the affair was settled to my satisfaction, except that the man somehow forgot to send the papers.

WE TOOK CHAMPION hunting for the first time at a gravel quarry where mergansers liked to congregate. These ducks were considered bad eating, so most people didn't shoot them. But Dwight would shoot at anything. He was a poor hunter, restless and unobservant and loud, and he never got the animals he went after. This made him furious; on the way back to the car he would kill anything he saw. He killed chipmunks, squirrels, blue jays and robins. He killed a great snowy owl with a 12-gauge from ten feet away and took potshots at bald eagles as they skimmed the river. I never saw him get a deer, a grouse, a quail, a pheasant, an edible duck, or even a large fish.

He thought his equipment was to blame. To his collection of target rifles he added two hunting rifles, a Marlin 30/30 and a Garand M-1 with a telescopic sight. He had a double-barreled 12-gauge shotgun for waterfowl and a semiautomatic 16-gauge that he called his "bush gun." To spot the game he never got close to he carried a pair of high-powered Zeiss binoculars. To dress the game he never killed he carried a Puma hunting knife.

For all the talk of Champion being my dog, I understood that he was supposed to be part of Dwight's total hunting system.

When we reached the quarry, Dwight threw a stick into the water to stimulate Champion's retrieving instincts and to demonstrate the softness of his mouth. He said weimaraners were famous for their mouths. "You won't see one tooth mark on that stick," he told me. Champion ran up to the water, then stopped. He looked back at us and whimpered. He was quaking like a chihuahua. "Go on, boy," Dwight said. Champion whimpered again. He bent one paw, stuck it in the water, pulled it out and started barking at the stick.

"Smart dog," Dwight said. "Knows it's not a bird."

The mergansers came in at dusk. They must have seen us, but as if they knew what they tasted like they showed no fear. They flew in low and close together. Dwight fired both barrels at them. One duck dropped like a stone and the rest rushed up again, quacking loudly. They circled the quarry long enough for Dwight to reload and fire. This time he didn't hit anything, and the mergansers flew away.

The bird he'd brought down was floating in the water about twenty feet from shore. Its bill was under the surface, its wings outstretched. It wasn't moving. Dwight broke the shotgun and pulled out the shells. "Get 'er, Champ," he said. But Champion did not get the duck. He wasn't even on the shore now, or anywhere else in sight. Dwight called to him in tones of friendliness, command, and threat, but he did not return. I offered to bring the duck in by throwing rocks behind it. Dwight said not to bother, it was just a garbage bird.

We found Champion under the car. Dwight had to sweet-talk him for several minutes before he bellied out, yelping softly and cowering. "He's a little gun-shy is all," Dwight said. "We can fix that."

Dwight decided to fix that by taking Champion goose hunting in eastern Washington. He talked my mother into going along. They were supposed to be away for about a week, but came back on unfriendly terms after three days. My mother told me that Champion had run off across the fields after the first shot, and that it took Dwight most of the afternoon to find him. They kept him in the car the next day but he pissed and crapped all over the seats. That was when they decided to come home.

"He cleaned it up," she added, "Every bit of it. I wouldn't go near it."

I hadn't asked. I guess she just thought I'd like to know.

CHAMPION DIDN'T ALWAYS growl when I came in. Usually he ignored me, and in time I would let down my guard, and then he would do it again and scare the hell out of me. One night he gave me such a fright that I grabbed a sponge mop and hit him over the head. Champion snarled and I hit him again and kept hitting him, screaming myself hysterical while he tried to get away, his paws scrabbling on the wooden floor.

Finally he stuck his head behind the water heater and kept it there as I worked the rest of him over. At some point I got tired, and saw what I was doing, and stopped.

I was alone in the house. I tried to pace off the jangling I felt, and the guilt. I could forgive myself for most things, but not cruelty.

I went back to the utility room. Champion was lying on his blanket again. I prodded his bones and examined him for cuts. He seemed okay. The sponge had taken the force of the blows. While I checked him over, Champion whined and licked my hands. I spoke gently to him. This was a mistake. It gave him the idea that I liked him, that we were pals. From that night on he wanted to be with me all the time. Whenever I passed through the utility room he groveled and abased himself, hoping to keep me there, then barked and hurled himself against the door as I went outside.

This caused me some trouble. For almost a year now, ever since I started high school, I'd been sneaking out of the house after midnight to take the car for joy rides. Dwight wouldn't teach me to drive—he claimed to believe that I would kill us both—so I had taken the teaching function upon myself. After Champion attached himself to me, I had to bring him along or he would raise the household with his cries.

With Champion beside me on the front seat, gazing out the window like a real passenger or snapping his chops at the wind, I cruised the empty streets of the camp. When I got bored I took the car to a stretch of road halfway to Marble-mount where I could get it up to a hundred miles an hour without having to make any turns. As Champion placidly watched the white line shivering between the headlights I chattered like a gibbon and wept tears of pure terror. Then I stopped the car in the middle of the road, turned it around, and did the same thing headed the other way. I drove a little farther each time. Someday, I thought, I would just keep going.

One morning I backed the car into a ditch while turning it around for my run home. I spun the wheels for a while, then got out and looked things over. I spun the wheels some more, until I was dug in good and deep. Then I gave up and started the trek back to camp. It was nearly three o'clock, and the walk home would take at least four hours. They would find me missing before I got there. The car too. I let off a string of swear words, but they seemed to be coming at me, not from me, and I soon stopped.

Champion ran ahead through the forest that crowded the road on both sides. The mountains were black all around, the stars brilliant in the inky sky. My footsteps were loud on the roadway. I heard them as if they came from somebody else. The movement of my legs began to feel foreign to me, and then the rest of my body, foreign and unconvincing, as if I were only pretending to be someone. I watched this body clomp along. I was outside it, watching it without belief. Its imitation of purpose seemed absurd and frightening. I did not know what it was, or what was watching it so anxiously, from so far away.

And then a voice bawled, "Oh Maybelline!" I knew that voice. It was mine, and it was loud, and I got behind it. I sang

"Maybelline" and another song, and another. I kept singing at the top of my voice. A couple of times I broke off to try to think up an excuse for my situation—Look, I know you won't believe this, but I just kind of woke up and there I was, *driving the car!*—but all of these ideas led me to despair, and I went back to singing songs. I sang every song I knew, and it began to amaze me how many of them there were. And I became aware that I didn't sound that bad out here where I could really cut loose—that I sounded pretty good. I took different parts. I did talking songs, like "Deck of Cards" and "Three Stars." I sang falsetto. I began to enjoy myself.

I WAS HALFWAY to Chinook when I heard an engine behind me. I faced the lights and flagged the driver down. He stopped his truck in the road, engine running, a man I didn't know. "That your car back there?" he asked.

I said it was.

"How'd you do that, anyway?"

"It's hard to explain," I said.

He told me to get in. I started yelling for Champion. "Wait a minute," he said. "Who's this Champ? You didn't say anything about any Champ."

"My dog."

The man peered into the darkness while I tried to call Champion in. He was afraid of what was out there and afraid of me, and his fear made me feel dangerous. Finally he said, "I'm going," but just then Champion bounded out of the trees. The man looked at him. "God almighty," he said, but he opened the door for us and drove us back to the car. He was silent during the drive and silent while he winched the car up onto the road. When I thanked him, he just nodded slightly and drove away.

I made it into bed not long before my mother came to wake me. "I don't feel so good," I told her.

She put her hand on my forehead, and at that gesture I wanted to tell her everything, the whole scrape, not by way of confession but in my exhilaration at having gotten out of it. She liked hearing stories about close calls; they confirmed her faith in luck. But I knew that I couldn't tell her without at least promising never to take the car again, which I had every intention of doing, or at worst forcing her to betray me to Dwight.

She looked down at me in the gray light of dawn. "You don't have a fever," she said. "But I have to admit, you look awful." She told me I could stay home from school that day if I promised not to watch TV.

I slept until lunchtime. I was sitting up in bed, eating a sandwich, when Dwight came to my room. He leaned in the doorway with his hands in his pockets like a mime acting out Relaxation. It made me wary.

"Feeling better?" he asked.

I said I was.

"Wouldn't want you to come down with anything serious," he said. "Get some sleep, did you?"

"Yes sir."

"You must've needed it."

I waited.

"Oh, by the way, you didn't happen to hear a funny little pinging noise in the engine, did you?"

"What engine?"

He smiled.

Then he said he'd been at the commissary a few minutes ago with Champion, and that he'd met a man there who recognized the dog and told a pretty interesting story of how they happened to cross paths earlier that morning. What did I think about that?

I said I didn't know what he was talking about.

Then he was on me. He caught me with one hand under the covers and the other holding the sandwich, and at first, instead of protecting myself, I jerked the sandwich away as if that was what he wanted. His open hands lashed back and forth across my face. I dropped the sandwich and covered my face with my forearm, but I couldn't keep his hands away. He was kneeling on the bed, his legs on either side of me, locking me in with the blankets. I shouted his name, but he kept hitting me in a fast convulsive rhythm and I knew he was beyond all hearing. Somehow, with no conscious intention, I pulled my other arm free and hit him in the throat. He reared back, gasping. I pushed him off the bed and kicked the covers away, but before I could get up he grabbed my hair and forced my face down hard against the mattress. Then he hit me in the back of the neck. I went rigid with the shock. He tightened his grip on my hair. I waited for him to hit me again. I could hear him panting. We stayed like that for a while. Then he pushed me away and got up. He stood over me, breathing hoarsely. "Clean up this mess," he said. He turned at the door and said, "I hope you learned your lesson."

I learned a couple of lessons. I learned that a punch in the throat does not always stop the other fellow. And I learned that it's a bad idea to curse when you're in trouble, but a good idea to sing, if you can.

CHAMPION HAD SEEN his last merganser. He turned out to be a cat killer. Three times he brought dead cats back to the house between those famously soft jaws of his. Dwight dropped them in the river and yelled at Pearl and me for letting him out. But Champ was under suspicion, and one day he got into someone's back yard and tore a Persian kitten to pieces under the eyes of the little girl who owned it. The camp director knocked on the door that evening and told Dwight that Champion had to go, now. Dwight said he'd need a few days to find him another home, but the camp director said that what he meant by now was *now*, as soon as he left.

Dwight stayed in the utility room for some time. After a spell of silence I heard him rummaging around. Then he said, "Come on, Champ." My mother and I were reading in the living room. We looked at each other. I went to the window and watched Dwight walking into the dusk, Champion sniffing the ground ahead of him. Dwight was carrying the 30/30. He let Champion into the car and drove away, upriver.

Dwight was only gone for a little while. I knew he hadn't buried Champion, because he came back so soon and because we didn't own a shovel.

My mother and I liked to watch *The Untouchables*. On one episode Al Capone confronted a man who had disappointed him. He listened to the man's tortured explanation with a look of sympathy and understanding. Then he said, softly, "Why don't you take a little ride with Frank?" The man's eyes bulged. He looked at Frank Nitti, then turned back to Al Capone and cried, "No, Mr. Capone, wait, I'll make it up to you . . ." But Mr. Capone was reading some papers on his desk. The next shot showed a long black car parked on a country road.

After Champion, whenever I did something wrong my mother would say to me, "Why don't you take a little ride with Dwight?"

Citizenship
in the School

Concrete was a company town, home of the Lone Star Cement Company. The streets and houses and cars were gray with cement dust from the plant. On still days a pall of dust hung in the air, so thick they sometimes had to cancel football practice. Concrete High overlooked the town from a hill whose slopes had been covered with cement to keep them from washing away. By the time I started there, not long after the school was built, its cement banks had begun to crack and slide, revealing the chicken wire over which they had been poured.

The school took students from up and down the valley. They were the children of farmers, waitresses, loggers, construction workers, truck drivers, itinerant laborers. Most of the boys already had jobs themselves. They worked not to save money but to spend it on their cars and girlfriends. Many of them got married while they were still in school, then dropped out to work full-time. Others joined the army or the marines—never the navy. A few became petty criminals. The boys of Concrete High tended not to see themselves as college material.

The school had some good teachers, mostly older women who didn't care if they were laughed at for reciting poetry, or for letting a tear fall while they described the Battle of Verdun. There were not many of them.

Mr. Mitchell taught civics. He also acted as unofficial recruiter for the army. He had served during World War II in "the European Theater," as he liked to say, and had actually killed men. He sometimes brought in different items he had taken from their bodies, not only medals and bayonets, which you could buy in any pawnshop, but also letters in German and wallets with pictures of families inside. Whenever we wanted to distract Mr. Mitchell from collecting essays we hadn't written, we would ask about the circumstances of his kills. Mr. Mitchell would crouch behind his desk, peer over the top, then roll into the middle of the room and spring to his feet yelling *da-da-da-da-da*. But he praised the courage and discipline of the Germans, and said that in his opinion we had fought on the wrong side. We should have gone into Moscow, not Berlin. As far as the concentration camps were concerned, we had to remember that nearly all the Jewish scientists had perished there. If they had lived, they would have helped Hitler develop his atomic bomb before we developed ours, and we would all be speaking German today.

Mr. Mitchell relied heavily on audiovisual aids in teaching his classes. We saw the same movies many times, combat documentaries and FBI-produced cautionary tales about high-school kids tricked into joining communist cells in Anytown, U.S.A. On our final examination Mr. Mitchell asked, "What is your favorite amendment?" We were ready for this question, and all of us gave the correct answer—"The Right to

Bear Arms"—except for a girl who answered "Freedom of Speech." For this impertinence she failed not only the question but the whole test. When she argued that she could not logically be marked wrong on this question, Mr. Mitchell blew up and ordered her out of the classroom. She complained to the principal but nothing came of it. Most of the kids in the class thought she was being a smarty-pants, and so did I.

Mr. Mitchell also taught PE. He had introduced boxing to the school, and every year he organized a smoker where hundreds of people paid good money to watch us boys beat the bejesus out of each other.

Miss Houlihan taught speech. She had adopted some years back a theory of elocution that had to do with "reaching down" for words rather than merely saying them, as if they were already perfectly formed in our stomachs and waiting to be brought up like trout from a stock pond. Instead of using our lips we were supposed to simply let the words "escape." This was hard to get the hang of. Miss Houlihan believed in getting the first thing right before moving on to the next, so we spent most of the year grunting "Hiawatha" in a choral arrangement she herself had devised. She liked it so much that in the spring she took us to a speech tournament in Mount Vernon. The competition was held outside, and it started to rain while we sat declaiming in The Great Circle. We wore Indian costumes made from burlap sacks that had once held onions. When the burlap got wet it started to stink. We were not the only ones to notice. Miss Houlihan wouldn't let us quit. She walked around behind the circle, whispering,

"Reach down, reach down." In the end we were disqualified for keeping time on a tom-tom.

Horseface Greeley taught shop. At the introductory class for each group of freshmen it was his custom to drop a fifty-pound block of iron on his foot. He did this as an attention-getter and to show off his Tuff-Top shoes, which had reinforced steel uppers. He thought we should all wear Tuff-Tops. We couldn't buy them in the stores but we could order them through him. When I was in my second year at Concrete an impetuous freshman tried to catch the block of iron as it fell toward Horseface's foot, and got his fingers crushed.

I BROUGHT HOME good grades at first. They were a fraud—I copied other kids' homework on the bus down from Chinook and studied for tests in the hallways as I walked from class to class. After the first marking period I didn't bother to do that much. I stopped studying altogether. Then I was given C's instead of A's, yet no one at home ever knew that my grades had fallen. The report cards were made out, incredibly enough, in pencil, and I owned some pencils myself.

All I had to do was go to class, and sometimes even that seemed too much. I had fallen in with some notorious older boys from Concrete who took me on as a curiosity when they discovered that I'd never been drunk and still had my cherry. I was grateful for their interest. I wanted distinction, and the respectable forms of it seemed to be eluding me. If I couldn't have it as a citizen I would have it as an outlaw.

We smoked cigarettes every morning in a shallow gully behind the school, and we often stayed there when the bell rang for class, then cut downhill through a field of ferns— ferns so tall we seemed to be swimming through them—to the side road where Chuck Bolger kept his car.

Chuck's father owned a big auto parts store near Van Horn and was also the minister of a Pentecostal church. Chuck himself talked dark religion when he was drinking. He was haunted and wild, but his manner was gentle; even, at least with me, brotherly. For that reason I felt easier with him than with the others. I believed that there were at least some things he would not do. I did not have that feeling about the rest. One of them had already spent time in jail, first for stealing a chain saw and then for kidnapping a cat. He was big and stupid and peculiar. Everyone called him Psycho and he had accepted the name like a vocation.

Chuck was with Psycho when he snatched the cat. The cat walked up to them while they were standing outside the Concrete drugstore and began to rub against their legs. Psycho picked the cat up to do it some injury, but when he saw the name on its collar he got an idea. The cat belonged to a widow whose husband had owned a car dealership in town. Psycho figured she must be loaded, and decided to put the arm on her. He called the widow from a pay phone and told her he had the cat and would sell it back to her for twenty dollars. Otherwise he would kill it. To show he meant business he held the cat up to the receiver and pulled its tail, but it wouldn't make any noise. Finally Psycho moved the receiver back to his own mouth and said, "Meow, meow." Then he told the widow to get the money and meet him at a certain place at a certain time. When Chuck tried to talk him out of going, Psycho called him a pussy. The widow wasn't there. Some other people were.

Then there was Jerry Huff. Huff was handsome in a pouty, heavy-lidded way. Girls liked him, which was bad luck for them. He was short but enormously strong and vain. His vanity crested above his head in a stupendous gleaming pompadour. He was a bully. He loitered in the bathrooms and made fun of other boys' dicks and stepped on their white buck shoes and held them over toilet bowls by their ankles. Bullies are supposed to be cowards but Huff confounded this wisdom. He would try to bully anyone, even guys who had already beaten him up.

Arch Cook also ran with us. Arch was an amiable simpleton who talked to himself and sometimes shouted or laughed for no reason. His head was long and thin and flat on the sides. Chuck told me that a car had driven over him when he was a baby. This was probably true. Huff used to tell him, "Arch, you might've been okay if that guy hadn't backed up to see what he hit." Arch was Huff's cousin.

There were five of us. We piled into Chuck's '53 Chevy and drove around looking for a car we could siphon gas out of. If we found one we emptied a few gallons from its tank into Chuck's and spent the morning tearing up the fire roads into the mountains. Around lunchtime we usually drove back down to Concrete and dropped in on Arch's sister Veronica. She'd been in Norma's class at Concrete. She still had the pert nose and wide blue eyes of the lesser Homecoming royalty she'd once been, but her face was going splotchy and loose from drink. Veronica was married to a sawyer who worked at a mill near Everett and came home only on the weekends. She had two fat little girls who wandered the wreckage of the house in their underpants, whining for their mother's attention and eating potato chips from economy packs almost as big as they were. Veronica was crazy about Chuck. If he wasn't in the mood, she would try to get him in the mood by walking around in short-shorts and high heels, or by sitting in his lap and sticking her tongue in his ear.

We hung around the house all afternoon, playing cards and reading Veronica's detective magazines. Now and then I tried to play games with the little girls, but they were too morose to pretend or imagine anything. At three o'clock I walked back up to Concrete High to catch my bus home.

CHUCK AND THE others knew a lot of women like Veronica, and girls on their way to being like Veronica. When they found a new one they shared her. They tried to fix me up with some of them, but I always backed out. I didn't know what these girls expected; I did know I was sure to disappoint them. Their availability unmanned me. And I didn't want it to be like that, squalid and public, with a stranger. I wanted it to be with the girl I loved.

This was not going to happen, because the girl I loved never knew I loved her. I kept my feelings secret because I believed she would find them laughable, even insulting. Her name was Rhea Clark. Rhea moved to Concrete from North Carolina halfway through her junior year, when I was a freshman. She had flaxen hair that hung to her waist, calm brown eyes, golden skin that glowed like a jar of honey. Her mouth was full, almost loose. She wore tight skirts that showed the flex and roll of her hips as she walked, clinging pastel sweaters whose sleeves she pushed up to her elbows, revealing a heartbreaking slice of creamy inner arm.

Just after Rhea came to Concrete I asked her to dance with me during a mixer in the gym. She nodded and followed me out onto the floor. It was a slow dance. When I turned to face her she moved into my arms as no other girl had ever done, frankly and fully. She melted against me and stayed against me, pliant to my least motion, her legs against mine, her cheek against mine, her fingers brushing the back of my neck. I understood that she didn't know who I was, that all of this was a new girl's mistake. But I felt justified in taking advantage of it. I thought we were meeting rightly, true self to true self, free of the accidents of age.

After a while she said, "Y'all don't know how to party."

Her voice was throaty and deep. I could feel it in my chest.

"Them old boys back in Norville could flat party," she said, "and that's no lie."

I couldn't speak. I just held her and moved her and breathed in her hair. I had her for three minutes and then I lost her forever. Older boys, boys I didn't have the courage to cut in on, danced with her the rest of the night. A week or so later she took up with Lloyd Sly, a basketball player with a hot car. When we passed in the hall she didn't even recognize me.

I wrote her long, grandiloquent letters which I then destroyed. I thought of the different ways that fate might put her in my power, so I could show her who I really was and make her love me. Most of these possibilities involved death or severe maiming for Lloyd Sly.

And when, as sometimes happened, a girl my own age showed some interest in me, I treated her swinishly. I walked her home from a dance or a game, made out with her on her front steps, then cut her dead the next day. I only ever wanted what I couldn't have.

CHUCK AND THE others had better luck getting me drunk. Though liquor disagreed with me they were patient, and willing to experiment, and time was on their side. They finally broke through during a basketball game, the last game of the season. It had rained earlier and the air was steamy. The windows of the school were open, and from our gully outside we could hear the cheerleaders warming up the people in the stands while the players did their layup drills.

> *Who's the team they hate to meet?*
> *Con-crete! Con-crete!*
> *Who's the team they just can't beat?*
> *Con-crete! Con-crete!*

Huff was passing around a can of Hawaiian Punch cut with vodka. Gorilla blood, he called it. I thought it would probably make me sick but I took a swig anyway. It stayed down. In fact I liked it, it tasted exactly like Hawaiian Punch. I took another swig.

I WAS UP on the school roof with Chuck. He was looking at me and nodding meditatively. "Wolff," he said. "Jack Wolff."

"Yo."

"Wolff, your teeth are too big."

"I know they are. I know they are."

"Wolf-man."

"Yo, Chuckles."

He held up his hands. They were bleeding. "Don't hit trees, Jack. Okay?"

I said I wouldn't.

"Don't hit trees."

I WAS LYING on my back with Huff kneeling on me, slapping my cheeks. He said, "Speak to me, dicklick," and I said, "Hi, Huff." Everybody laughed. Huff's pompadour had come unstuck and was hanging in long strands over his face. I smiled and said, "Hi, Huff."

*   *   *

I WAS WALKING along a branch. I was way out on it, over the far lip of the gully where the cement bank began. They were all looking up at me and yelling. They were fools, my balance was perfect. I bounced on the branch and flapped my arms. Then I put my hands in my pockets and strolled out along the branch until it broke.

I didn't feel myself land, but I heard the wind leave me in a rush. I was rolling sideways down the hillside with my hands still in my pockets, rolling around and around like a log, faster and faster, picking up speed on the steep cement. The cement ended in a drop where the earth below had washed away. I flew off the edge and went spinning through the air and landed hard and rolled downhill through the ferns, bouncing over rocks and deadfall, the ferns rustling around me, and then I hit something hard and stopped cold.

I was on my back. I could not move, I could not breathe. I was too empty to take the first breath, and my body would not respond to the bulletins I sent. Blackness came up from the bottom of my eyes. I was drowning, and then I drowned.

WHEN I OPENED my eyes I was still on my back. I heard voices calling my name but I did not answer. I lay amidst a profusion of ferns, their fronds glittering with raindrops. The fronds made a lattice above me. The voices came closer and still I did not answer. I was happy where I was. There was movement in the bushes all around me, and again and again I heard my name. I bit the inside of my cheek so I wouldn't laugh and give myself away, and finally they left.

I spent the night there. In the morning I walked down to the main road and thumbed a ride home. My clothes were wet and torn, but except for a certain tenderness down the length of my back I was unhurt, just creaky from my night on the ground.

Dwight was at the kitchen table when I came in. He looked me over and said—quietly, he knew he had me this time—"Where were you last night?"

I said, "I got drunk and fell off a cliff."

He grinned in spite of himself, just as I knew he would. He let me off with a lecture and some advice about hangovers while my mother stood by the sink in her bathrobe, listening without expression. After Dwight dismissed me she followed me down the hall. She stopped in my doorway, arms crossed, and waited for me to look at her. Finally she said, "You're not helping anymore."

NO, BUT I was happy that night, listening to them search for me, listening to them call my name. I knew they wouldn't find me. After they went away I lay there smiling in my perfect place. Through the ferns above me I saw the nimbus of the moon in the dense, dark sky. Cool beads of water rolled down the ferns onto my face. I could just make out the sounds of the game going on up the hill, the cheers, the drumming of feet in the stands. I listened with godly condescension. I was all alone where no one could find me, only the faint excitements of a game and some voices crying Concrete, Concrete, Concrete.

My brother and I hadn't seen each other in six years. After leaving Salt Lake I lost touch with him until, in the fall of my second year at Concrete High, he wrote me a letter and sent me a Princeton sweatshirt. The letter was full of impressive phrases—"In a world where contraception and the hydrogen bomb usurp each other as negative values . . ."—that I tried to use in conversation as if they had just occurred to me. I wore the sweatshirt everywhere, and told strangers who picked me up on the road that I was a Princeton student coming home for a visit. I even had my hair cut in a style called "The Princeton"—flat on top, long and swept back on the sides.

I decided to make my way there. My mother was busy campaigning for Senator Jackson and John F. Kennedy. Dwight called Kennedy "the Pope's candidate" and "the senator from Rome." He didn't like him, possibly because of his effect on my mother, who was stirred by Kennedy's hopefulness and also a little in love with him. With her out of the house so much Dwight had grown casual about pushing me around. He didn't really beat me but he kept the possibility alive. I hated being alone with him.

216

My idea was to hitchhike to Princeton and hand myself over to Geoffrey. I had no money for the trip. To get it, I planned to forge a check. For some time I had been struck by the innocence of banks, the trusting way they left checkbooks out on the service tables for their customers. People walked in off the street, wrote down their wishes, then walked out again with their pockets full of money. There was nothing to keep me from taking a few blanks to fill out later. I couldn't cash them in Chinook or Concrete, where I was too familiar to use a false name, but in another town it would be easy.

I belonged to the Order of the Arrow, a Scout honor society whose annual banquet was to be held in Bellingham that year. I drove down in the afternoon with some other OA members from my troop, and shook loose from them soon after we arrived. First I went to a bank. Before going inside I put on the horn-rimmed glasses my mother had bought me so I could see the blackboards at school. They made me look owlish, but older. I walked across the bank to one of the tables and tore off a check from the convenience checkbook. I waited in line for a while, then, snapping my fingers as if I had just remembered something, turned on my heels and walked back outside.

At the main branch of the public library I took out a card in the name of Thomas Findon. I chose "Thomas Findon" because I'd worked as a camp counselor with a boy of that name during the summer. He was an Eagle Scout from Portland, a soft-spoken athlete with the body of a man and an easy way with the girls who came to camp to visit their little brothers. We taught swimming together until I got demoted to the archery range, where I almost lost my job altogether for arranging twenty-five-cent matches with the young Scouts I was supposed to be teaching.

The library was as simple as the bank. All I had to do was give the librarian my name, and an address I'd copied at random from the telephone book. She typed up the card while I waited.

I WALKED THE streets for over an hour, looking at stores, at the people behind the counters. I was searching for someone I could trust. I found her in a corner drugstore in the business section, just up the street from the Swedish Sailors' Home. For several minutes I walked back and forth and watched her through the drugstore window. Then I went inside and stood by the magazine racks, pretending to read and nervously shifting my overnight bag from shoulder to shoulder. She was gray-haired but her face was smooth, her expression direct and open as a young girl's. A guileless, lovely face. She wore half-moon glasses that she peered over to look at her customers while she rang up their purchases. Afterward she passed the time with them, mostly listening but sometimes adding a comment of her own. Her laugh was soft and pleasant. She made the store like a home.

I picked up copies of *The Saturday Evening Post* and *Reader's Digest*, then prowled the aisle for other adult items.

I collected some Old Spice aftershave, brass-plated fingernail clippers, a hairbrush, and a package of pipe tobacco. As I approached the cash register she smiled and asked me how I was today.

"Grand," I said "just grand."

She added up my bill and asked if I wanted anything else.

"I believe that will do the trick," I said. I put my hand in my right rear pocket and frowned. Still frowning, I patted my other pockets. "Wouldn't you know it," I said. "I seem to have left my wallet at home. Drat! Sorry for the inconvenience."

She refused my offer to return the merchandise to the shelves and told me not to worry, it happened all the time. I thanked her and turned away, then turned back. "I could write you a check," I said. "Do you accept checks?"

"We sure do."

"Terrific." I produced the check I'd taken from the bank and laid it on the counter. "I'll make it out for fifty if that's all right."

She hesitated. "Fifty should be fine."

She watched me fill the check out. I had seen Dwight do it and knew the tricks, like writing "fifty and no/100" on the amount line. I signed it with a flourish and handed it to her.

She studied it. I waited, smiling patiently. When she spoke, her voice had changed somehow. "Thomas," she said, "do you have any identification?"

"Of course," I said, and reached for my rear pocket again. Then I stopped. "That darn wallet," I said. "It's all in there. I don't know, maybe I've got something." I searched through all my pockets, and with a show of relief I discovered the library card. "There we go," I said. "Now we're back in business."

She studied the card as she had studied the check. "Where do you live, Thomas?"

"Sorry?"

She looked at me over her glasses. "What's your address?"

I had utterly forgotten what the card said. I stood there, blinking stupidly, then I leaned over the counter and plucked the card from her fingers and said, "It's right here." I read the address to her and handed the card back.

She nodded, watching me. Then she raised her head and called out, "Albert, could you come here a minute?"

A short, frail old man in a white jacket came slowly down the aisle from the prescription desk. She handed him the check and library card. She fixed her eyes on him and said in a deliberate voice, "Albert, the young man here wrote us this check. Take care of it, please." He looked at her, uncertainly at first, then with some sharpness. "Right," he said. "I'll take care of it." He walked back down the aisle. I began to follow him but she said, "He'll be right back, Thomas. Just wait here."

She put my purchases in a bag and we stood without speaking for a time. "I don't usually keep that much cash on hand," she finally said.

I looked toward the rear of the store. I couldn't see the man.

"So how long have you been living here, Thomas?"

"About six months," I said.

"And how do you like it so far?"

"Okay. I mean I really like it."

"Good. I do too, it's a nice place to live. People here are nice."

Then I saw that she was trembling, close to tears, and I knew she had betrayed me. I glanced toward the empty prescription desk again and said, "You know, I've got some other things to do, I'll just come back later."

I started down the aisle. She said, "Wait, Thomas." When I reached the door I looked around and saw that she had come from behind the counter and was following me. "Wait," she said, holding me with her eyes as I stood there, and I saw in her eyes what I had heard in her voice earlier: sorrow. I pulled the door open and stepped outside and began walking fast down the street. I passed a few shops and then I heard her voice behind me again— "Thomas!" I quickened my pace. She kept following and calling out to me. I looked over my shoulder. She was running, slowly and clumsily, but running. I squeezed the overnight bag against my side with my elbow and broke into a run myself. The two of us ran down the street, twenty, twenty-five feet apart. I was holding back, just loping along. "Thomas!" she said, "Thomas, wait!" and every time she spoke I felt a tug from this voice so full of care. I felt she knew all of me, all my foolishness and trouble, and wanted only to take hold of me and set me right.

The sidewalk was crowded. If the men and women we ran through had thought there was any reason to stop me, they would have. If she had yelled "Thief!" just once, I would have been mobbed on the spot. Everyone must have thought it was a family affair. They must have heard what I heard, the voice of a mother trying to reach her child.

I turned the corner at the end of the block, and this somehow broke her hold on me. All the speed I'd been saving seemed to come to me at once. I tore down to the next corner, turned, turned again half a block later and ran through an alley. Only then did I slow down and look behind me. She could not possibly have kept up, but I needed to look to be sure. She wasn't there. I had lost her. I believed I had lost her forever, but in this I was mistaken.

The alley ended across the street from a diner. The street was under repair. No cars, only a few pedestrians. I waited for a time, trying to get my wind back, then crossed over to the diner. It was almost empty. The cashier grunted when I came in but didn't look up from the tablet he was writing on. I walked to the back and locked myself in the men's room.

I leaned against the door. I stood there, just letting myself breathe. My eyes burned with sweat and my shirt was soaked through. My throat was raw. I bent my head to the faucet and let the water run into my mouth. Then I stripped to the waist and bathed myself with paper towels. When I was dry, I took off my pants and stuffed them into the overnight bag with my shirt and my glasses. I took out my Boy Scout uniform and slowly, carefully, unfolded it and put it on. I ran a damp tissue over my shoes, then straightened up and inspected myself. Everything was as it should be, the set of my scarf, the alignment of my belt buckle, the angle of my cap, the drape of my two sashes. One was the Order of the Arrow sash, a red arrow on a brilliant white background. The other was my merit-badge sash. It was thick with proofs of competence. At camp that summer, with little else to do, I had worked myself into a delirium of badge-grubbing. I was a Life Scout now, with only one merit badge to go for Eagle. That badge was Citizenship in the Nation. I had already fulfilled the numerous requirements for it, including attendance at a jury trial to observe the rule of law, but Dwight refused to send in my papers. He wouldn't explain why, except to say I didn't deserve to be an Eagle. It was an issue between us.

I shouldered my bag and left the diner.

BETWEEN MY FLIGHT from the drugstore and my return, no more than fifteen minutes had gone by. An empty police car was parked outside the store with its light blinking. Calmly, eyes front and center, I walked past and up the street to the hotel where the banquet was to take place.

Though an hour remained until chow time the lobby was already full of Scouts in OA sashes, preening themselves and looking each other over. I checked my bag and said hello to some acquaintances from other troops. One of them was in charge of setting up chairs. He asked me to help him out, and when that job was done he posted me at the door with a couple of other boys to greet the guests as they arrived. The three of us sparked each other. By the time people began filing past our table we were laying down a steady line of scintillant repartee. Between gags I checked off names on the invitation list, the second boy wrote them down on adhesive nameplates, and the third escorted the guests to their tables.

Then she was there, in line behind an old couple. I looked up and saw her watching me. The room bucked but I kept my balance. I didn't even blink. I checked off the old couple's name, and made a friendly joke they laughed at.

And then I turned to her. I gave her a welcoming smile and said, "Name, ma'am?" She stepped up to the table and stood there thoughtfully, holding her pocketbook in front of her with both hands. She still had on the white sweater and plaid skirt she'd been wearing in the store. I felt no fear, nor any surprise after the first shock had passed. I knew she hadn't followed me here. Of course she would have a boy in the Scouts, and of course he would belong to OA. She read my nameplate and looked me up and down, and I could see her face grow smooth and serene as she decided that she had been mistaken, that it couldn't possibly be me. She returned my smile and gave me her name. I saw from the list that she had two boys in the Order. Already she was searching for them, glancing around her and peering into the noisy hall. She picked up her nameplate, gave her arm to the boy at the door, and passed into the banquet.

My brother sent me a story he had written called "A Hank o' Hair, A Piece of Bone." It was about an American imprisoned in Italy for murdering a prostitute. His father was rich, but the young man refused to ask him for help. He was alienated from his father and from everyone else. He was so alienated that he wouldn't even say he was sorry for killing the girl. He *was* sorry—he'd been drunk at the time—but such was his contempt for society that he would do nothing to court its mercy. The story was filled with closely observed details of prison life, such as automatic toilets flushing every few minutes and inmates banging on their bars with tin cups.

I thought it was great. I couldn't get over Geoffrey's audacity in writing it. I sent him one of mine, a story about two wolves fighting to the death in the Yukon, but I knew his was better and contemplated submitting it to my English teacher as if it were my own. In the end I decided not to. I knew I'd never get away with it.

Geoffrey wrote again to say he had liked my story and wanted me to send more. His letter was affectionate and full of news. This was his last year at Princeton. He hoped to move to Europe when he graduated, to work on a novel. There was also the possibility of a teaching job in Turkey. Princeton had

225

been good to him, he said, and I ought to give it some serious consideration when the time came to choose my own college.

Geoffrey also sent word of my father. He and his wife were separated. He had moved to California and found work at Convair Astronautics, the first real job he had had in years. In fact, Geoffrey said, they'd all been having a bumpy time of it for quite a while now. He would tell me more when he saw me, which he hoped to do before he left the country. It had been too long, he said.

Geoffrey wanted to see me. That was plain. I had been wanting to see him for years, but before now, even when I hatched plans to join up with him, I never knew whether he felt the same way. In most respects we were strangers. But it mattered to me that he was my brother, and it seemed to matter to him. In his letters, elegance of tone had given way to simple friendliness. I carried the letters around with me and read them with elation.

DWIGHT CAME INTO the kitchen one afternoon while Pearl and I were eating some hot dogs I'd cooked up. He noticed a jar of French's mustard in the garbage pail and fished it out. "Who threw this away?" he asked.

I told him I had.

"Why did you throw it away?"

"Because it was empty."

"Because it was *empty*? Does this look empty to you?"

He held the bottle close to my face. There were a few streaks of mustard congealed under the neck and in the grooves at the bottom.

Pearl said, "It looks empty to me."

"I didn't ask you," Dwight told her.

"Well, it does," she said.

I said that it looked empty to me, too.

"Look again," he said, and pushed the open neck of the jar against my eye. When I jerked away he grabbed me by the hair and shoved my face back down toward the jar. "Does this look empty to you?"

I didn't answer.

"Dad," Pearl said.

He asked me again if the jar looked empty. It was hurting my eye, so I said no, it didn't look empty. He let go of me. "Clean it out," he said. He handed me the jar. I picked up a knife and began scraping at the mustard while he watched. After a time he sat down across the table. The streaks were hard to get at, especially under the neck where the knife wouldn't go. Dwight grew impatient. He said, "You're going to have to do better than that if you think you're ever going to be an engineer."

Back in the days when Skipper talked of going to engineering school I had insincerely declared the same ambition, hoping to pick up some points by echoing his sober program. The more I said it the more possible it seemed. I had no interest in the specifics of the profession, and no aptitude, but my father was an engineer and I liked the sound of the word.

I got out as much of the mustard as I could. It made a brown and yellow smudge where I'd scraped it off on the edge of my plate.

"All right," Dwight said. "Now—was it empty?"

"Yes," I said.

He leaned across the table and slapped my face. He didn't swing hard but the slap was loud. Pearl started yelling at him, and while he was yelling back I got up and left the house. I wandered around feeling sorry for myself. Then I decided to buy a Coke from the machine on the loading ramp of the main warehouse. There was also a phone booth on the ramp, and as I drank the Coke I formed the idea of calling my brother. I didn't know how to do it, but the operator was amused by my helplessness and steered me through. She got Geoffrey's number from Princeton information, then calmed me when I panicked at her request for money. "We'll just make it collect," she said. I listened to the muffled signal ring through the static. I was quaking. And then I heard his voice. I had not heard it for six years, but I knew it right away. He accepted the call and said, "Hello, Toby."

I tried to say hello back but the word got stuck in my throat. Every time I tried to speak I seized up again. It wasn't self-pity; it was hearing my brother's voice and, for the first time in all these years, the sound of my own name. But I couldn't explain any of this. Geoffrey kept asking me what was wrong, and when I found my voice I told him the first thing that came to mind—that Dwight had hit me.

"He hit you! What do you mean, he hit you?"

It took me a while to get the story out. The word *mustard* resists serious treatment, and as I described what had happened I began to fear that Geoffrey would find the episode ridiculous, so I made it sound worse than it had been.

Geoffrey listened without interrupting me. Once I was finished he said, "Let me get this straight. He hit you because of a little mustard?"

I said that he had.

"Where was Mom?"

"Working."

Geoffrey was quiet for a moment. When he spoke again he sounded discouraged. "Toby, I don't know what to say."

"I just thought I'd call," I said.

"Wait a minute," he said. "He had no right to hit you like that. Has he done it before?"

I said he had—"all the time."

"That's it, then," Geoffrey said. "You've got to get out of there."

I asked if I could come live with him.

"No," he said. "That wouldn't be possible."

"What about Dad?"

"No, you don't want to live with the old man right now, believe me." Geoffrey said he had something else in mind, something he'd been planning to mention the next time he wrote. He asked me what the school was like in Chinook. When I told him I went forty miles downriver to the high school in Concrete, he said, *"Where?"*

"Concrete."

"Concrete. Jesus. What are they teaching you?"

I listed my courses. Band, shop, algebra, PE, English, civics, and driver's ed. Geoffrey made unhappy sounds. When he asked about my grades I told him I was getting straight A's. "That's good," he said. "That gives us something to go on. You're obviously doing as well as you can, and that's what they'll be looking for."

Then he told me what he had in mind. He said that his old prep school, Choate, awarded a certain number of scholarships every year. Given the fact that I was earning top grades, he thought I might have a chance at one of these scholarships. It was a long shot, but why not try? I should also apply to Deerfield, where our father had gone for a time, and to St. Paul's. Maybe some others. They liked jocks, he said. Was I a jock?

I told him I was a swimmer.

"Good, they *love* swimmers. You swim for your school?"

"The school doesn't have a team. I swim for my Scout troop."

"You're a Scout? Great! Better and better. What rank?"

"Eagle."

He laughed. "Christ, Toby, they'll be eating out of your hand. Anything else? Chess? Music?"

"I play in the school band."

"Terrific. What instrument?"

"Snare drum."

"Yes, well, let's stick with the grades and swimming and the Scouts." Geoffrey told me he would send a list of schools to apply to, along with addresses and deadlines. I would have to be patient, this wasn't going to happen overnight. "I don't like the idea of that guy hitting you," Geoffrey said. "Think you can hang on out there?"

I said I could.

"I'm going to call the old man about this. He might have some ideas. We'll get you out of there, one way or the other." He told me to give his love to our mother, and to keep writing. He said he really liked the wolf story.

THIS WAS A low time for my mother. During the campaign she had traveled up and down the valley, and gone to conventions, and spent her time with people she admired. She had met John F. Kennedy. Now that the election was over she'd gone back to waiting tables at the cookhouse. She missed the excitement, but her sadness went beyond that, beyond boredom and fatigue. She had told a man who'd worked with her on the campaign that she wanted to get out of Chinook, and he offered to pull some strings to find her a job back East. Dwight somehow got wind of it. While they were driving up from Marblemount one night, he turned off on a logging road and took her to a lonely place. She asked him to go back but he refused to say anything. He just sat there, drinking from a bottle of whiskey. When it was empty he pulled his hunting knife out from under the seat and held it to her throat. He kept her there for hours like that, making her beg for her life, making her promise that she would never leave him. If she left him, he said, he would find her and kill her. It didn't matter where she went or how long it took him, he would kill her. She believed him.

I knew something had happened, but I didn't know what. My mother wouldn't tell me. She was afraid I would make things worse if I knew, stir Dwight up all over again. The fact was, she had no money and no place to go. Alone, she might have bolted anyway. With me to take care of she thought she couldn't.

When I told her I'd spoken to Geoffrey, her eyes filled with tears. This was unusual for her. We were sitting at the kitchen table, where we liked to talk when we were alone in the house. Geoffrey had recently been sending my mother letters, too, but they hadn't spoken since we left Utah. She wanted to know what he sounded like, how he was, and all manner of things I had not thought to ask him. My mother grew somber, as she often did when we talked about Geoffrey. She was afraid she'd done the wrong thing in letting him go with my father, afraid he held it against her, that and the divorce, and taking up with Roy.

I mentioned Geoffrey's idea about Choate, about the possibility of my getting a scholarship there or maybe at some other school. I was afraid of her reaction. I thought she would be hurt by my wish to go, but she liked the idea. "He actually thinks you have a chance?" she said.

"He said they'll be eating out of my hand, quote unquote."

"I don't know why he thinks that."

"My grades are good," I said.

"That's true. Your grades are good. What other schools did he mention?"

"St. Paul's."

"He's got big plans for you."

"Deerfield."

She laughed. "They'll recognize your name, anyway. I think your father was the only boy they ever expelled." Then she said, "Don't get your hopes too high."

"Geoffrey said he'd talk to Dad about it. He said maybe Dad would have some ideas."

"I'm sure he will," she said.

GEOFFREY SENT THE names and addresses of the schools he had first mentioned, and also three others—Hill, Andover, and Exeter. I went to the library at school and looked them up in Vance Packard's *The Status Seekers*. This book explained how the upper class perpetuates itself. Its motive was supposedly democratic, to attack snobbery and subvert the upper class by giving away its secrets. But I didn't read it as social criticism. To seek status seemed the most natural thing in the world to me. Everyone did it. The people who bought the book were certainly doing it. They consulted it with the same purpose I had, not to deplore the class problem but to solve it by changing classes.

Whatever he meant it to be, Packard's book was the perfect guide for social climbers. He listed the places you should live and the colleges you should go to and the clubs you should join and the faith you should confess. He named the tailors and stores you should patronize, and described with filigree exactitude the ways you could betray your origins. Wearing a blue serge suit to a yacht-club party. Saying davenport for sofa, ill for sick, wealthy for rich. Painting the walls of your house in bright colors. Mixing ginger ale with whiskey. Being too good a dancer. He showed boxes within boxes, circles within circles. Of course you would go to an Ivy League school, but that by itself wouldn't do the trick. "The point is not Harvard, but which Harvard? By Harvard one means Porcellian, Fly, or AD." And he said that the key to which Harvard one attended, or which Yale, or which Princeton, and therefore which life one led thereafter, was one's prep school. "Harvard or Yale or Princeton is not enough. It is the really exclusive prep school that counts. . . ."

Packard said there were over three thousand private schools in America. Only a very few satisfied his standard of exclusivity. He specified them in a brief list almost exactly the same as Geoffrey's. I understood, pondering these names in the library of Concrete High, that the brilliant life they promised depended on leaving most people out, to loud walls and bad tailors. I did not want to be left out. Now that I had felt the possibility of this life, any other life would be an oppression.

Packard made a point of saying that these schools were just about impossible for outsiders to get into. But he did mention that they gave scholarships, and that many of the scholarships went to "descendants of once-prosperous alumni who had come into difficult times." That made me feel as if the people at Deerfield were just sitting around waiting to hear from me.

I wrote off for application forms. The schools responded quickly, with cover letters in whose stiff courtesy I managed to hear panting enthusiasm. I did get a friendly note from John Boyden, the headmaster of Deerfield and the son of the man who had thrown my father out. He said that the school was already swamped with applications that year, and recommended that I apply to some other schools. His list was familiar. In a handwritten postscript he added that he remembered my father, and wished me all the best. I fixed on this cordial nod as a signal of favor.

When the forms were all in, I sat down to fill them out and ran into a wall. I could see from the questions they asked that to get into one of these schools, let alone win a scholarship, I had to be at least the boy I'd described to my brother and probably something more. Geoffrey was willing to take me at my word; the schools were not. Each of the applications required supporting letters. They wanted letters from teachers, coaches, counselors, and, if possible, their own alumni. They asked for an account of my Community Service, and left a space of disheartening length for the answer. Likewise Athletic Achievements, likewise Foreign Travel, and Languages. I understood that these claims were to be confirmed in the letters of recommendation. They wanted my grades sent by Concrete High on its official transcript form. Finally, they required that I take a prep-school version of the Scholastic

Aptitude Test, to be administered in January at the Lakeside School in Seattle.

I was stumped. Whenever I looked at the forms I felt despair. Their whiteness seemed hostile and vast, Saharan. I had nothing to get me across. During the day I composed high-flown circumlocutions, but at night, when it came to writing them down, I balked at their silliness. The forms stayed clean. When my mother pressed me to send them off, I transferred them to my locker at school and told her everything was taken care of. I did not trouble my teachers for praise they could not give me, or bother to have my collection of C's sent out. I was giving up— *being realistic*, as people liked to say, meaning the same thing. Being realistic made me feel bitter. It was a new feeling, and one I didn't like, but I saw no way out.

MY FATHER CALLED. He called on a night when both Dwight and Pearl were out of the house, and that was a lucky thing, because my mother took the call and everything about her immediately changed. She became girlish. I realized who it was and stood beside her, straining to hear words in the rumble of my father's voice. He did most of the talking. My mother smiled and shook her head. Now and then she laughed skeptically and said, "We'll have to see," and "I don't know about that." Finally she said, "He's right here," and handed the receiver over to me.

"Hi, Chum," he said, and I could feel him there. His bearish bulk, his tobacco smell.

I said hello.

"Your brother tells me you're thinking of Choate," he said. "Personally, I think you'd be happier at Deerfield."

"Well, I just applied," I said. "Maybe I won't get in."

"Oh, you'll get in all right, boy like you." He recited back to me the things I had told Geoffrey.

"I don't know. They get a lot of applications."

"You'll get in," he said sternly. "The question is, which school to choose. I'm simply suggesting that Deerfield may be on a more congenial scale than Choate. Let's face it, you're used to being a big fish in a small pond—you might get lost at Choate. But it's your choice to make. If you want to go to Choate, for Christ's sake go to Choate! It's a fine school. A damn fine school."

"Yes sir."

He asked me where else I'd applied and I went through the list. He gave his approval, then added, "Mind you, Andover's something of a factory. I'm not sure I'd send a boy of mine there, but we can talk about that when the time comes. Now here's the plan."

The plan was that I should come down to La Jolla as soon as school was over. Then Geoffrey would fly out from Princeton after graduation and the three of us would spend the whole summer together. Geoffrey would work on his novel while I started preparing for classes at Deerfield. When we wanted a break we could go for a swim at Wind and Sea Beach, which was just down the street from the apartment. And later, when she saw how well everything was going, my mother would join us. We would be a family again. "I've made some mistakes," he told me. "We all have. But that's behind us. Right, Tober?"

"Right."

"You damn betcha. We're starting from scratch. And look, no more of this Jack business. You can't go off to Deerfield with a name like Jack. Understand?"

I said I understood.

"Good boy." He asked if it was true that my stepfather had hit me. When I said yes, he said, "The next time he does it, kill him." Then he asked to speak to my mother again.

After she hung up I told her what he'd said to me.

"Sounds real nice," she said. "Don't bank on it."

"He said you would come too."

"Hah! That's what he thinks. I'd have to be crazy to do that." Then she said, "Let's see what happens."

MY MOTHER DROVE me down to Seattle for the tests. I took the verbal section in the morning and immediately began to enjoy myself. I recognized, behind the easyseeming questions on vocabulary and reading comprehension, a competitive intelligence out to tempt me with answers that were not correct. The tricks had a smugness about them that provoked me. I wanted to confound these sharpies, show them I wasn't as dumb as they thought I was. When the monitor called the tests in I felt suddenly alone, as if someone had walked out on me in the middle of a good argument.

The other boys who were taking the test gathered in the hallway to compare answers. They all seemed to know each other. I did not approach them, but I watched them closely. They wore rumpled sport coats and baggy flannel pants. White socks showing above brown loafers. I was the only boy there in a suit, a salt-and-pepper suit I'd gotten for eighth-grade graduation, now too small for me. And I was the only boy there with a "Princeton" haircut. The others had long hair roughly parted and left hanging down across their foreheads, almost to their eyes. Now and then they tossed their heads to throw the loose hair back. The effect would have been careless on just one of them, but it was uniform, an effect of style, and I took note of it. I also took note of the way they talked to each other, their predatory, reflexive sarcasm. It interested me, excited me; at certain moments I had to make an effort not to laugh. As they spoke they smiled ironically, and rocked on their heels, and tossed their heads like nickering horses.

After lunch I walked around the campus. The regular students had not yet returned from their Christmas vacation, and the quiet was profound. I found a bench overlooking the lake. The surface was misty and gray. Until they rang the bell for the math test I sat with crossed legs and made believe I belonged here, that these handsome old buildings, webbed with vines of actual ivy to which a few brown leaves still clung, were my home.

ARTHUR HATED SHOP, which was a required course for boys at Concrete High. After making his eighth or ninth cedar box he revolted. He was able to negotiate his way out by agreeing to work in the school office during that period. I thought he would help me, but he refused angrily. His anger made no sense to me. I did not understand that he wanted out, too. I backed off and didn't ask again.

But a few days later he came up to me in the cafeteria, dropped a manila folder on the table, and walked away without a word. I got up and took the folder to the bathroom and locked myself in a stall. It was all there, everything I had asked for. Fifty sheets of school stationary, several blank transcript forms, and a stack of official envelopes. I slipped them into the folder again and went back to the cafeteria.

Over the next couple of nights I filled out the transcripts and the application forms. Now the application forms came easy; I could afford to be terse and modest in my self-descriptions, knowing how detailed my recommenders were going to be. When these were done I began writing the letters of support. I wrote out rough copies in longhand, then typed up the final versions on official stationary, using different machines in the typing lab at school. I wrote the first drafts deliberately, with much crossing out and penciling in, but with none of the hesitance I'd felt before. Now the words came as easily as if someone were breathing them into my ear. I felt full of things that had to be said, full of stifled truth. That was what I thought I was writing—the truth. It was truth known only to me, but I believed in it more than I believed in the facts arrayed against it. I believed that in some sense not factually verifiable I was a straight-A student. In the same way, I believed that I was an Eagle Scout, and a powerful swimmer, and a boy of integrity. These were ideas about myself that I had held on to for dear life. Now I gave them voice.

I made no claims that seemed false to me. I did not say that I was a star quarterback or even a varsity football player, because even though I went out for football every year I never quickened to the lumpen spirit of the sport. The same was true of basketball. I couldn't feature myself sinking a last-second clincher from the key, as Elgin Baylor did for Seattle that year in the NCAA playoffs against San Francisco. Ditto school politics; the unending compulsion to test one's own popularity was baffling to me.

These were not ideas I had of myself, and I did not propose to urge them on anyone else.

I declined to say I was a football star, but I did invent a swimming team for Concrete High. The coach wrote a fine letter for me, and so did my teachers and the principal. They didn't gush. They wrote plainly about a gifted, upright boy who had already in his own quiet way exhausted the resources of his school and community. They had done what they could for him. Now they hoped that others would carry on the good work.

I wrote without heat or hyperbole, in the words my teachers would have used if they had known me as I knew myself. These were their letters. And on the boy who lived in their letters, the splendid phantom who carried all my hopes, it seemed to me I saw, at last, my own face.

A rthur and I had fallen into a sharp way of talking to each other. It was supposed to be banter, but it turned easily cruel and sometimes led to shoving matches, grunting, scuffling affairs during which we smiled fixedly to show how little of our strength we were using. We started doing this after school one day while we were at the bus stop. It would have played itself out as usual except that some other boys took an interest and began shouting encouragement. This in turn attracted the attention of Mr. Mitchell, who ran across the street yelling, "Break it up! Break it up!" He came between us and held us apart as if we were slavering to get at each other.

"Okay," he said, "what's the problem here?"

Neither of us answered. I knew exactly what was going to happen, and that nothing I could say would change it.

"You don't fight on school property," Mr. Mitchell told us. "If you've got a grudge, I've got the place to work it out." He took out his notebook, wrote down our names, and congratulated us on volunteering for the smoker.

MR. MITCHELL HAD started the smokers some years back to showcase the boxing talent of a few boys, and his own talent

243

as their coach, but since then they had become big business. The tickets cost three dollars and sold out in a matter of days. This didn't happen because the quality of the fights got better, but because they got worse. Nobody wanted to see artful flyweights dance up and down, moving their shoulders prettily while darting in for another scientific love tap. They wanted to see slope-shouldered bruisers stand toe to toe and pound each other into goulash. They wanted to see blood. They wanted to see pain.

Mr. Mitchell gave it to them. The smokers turned into brawls. He matched up the hardest cases he could find, and he did not trouble himself overmuch with questions of height and weight. A mismatch could be just as much fun as an even match. More fun. You couldn't help but be interested in watching some jiggling fatty like Bull Slatter—Full Bladder, as he was known—defend his farflung borders against the malice of a brutal pygmy like Huff. Style wasn't the issue here. The folks wanted action, and the best action of the night happened in the grudge fights.

The grudge fights came last. Mr. Mitchell announced them as such to raise the temperature in the gym, and to remind the fighters that they were honor-bound to try and kill each other. Most of these boys weren't real enemies. Maybe they'd ragged each other too hard, like Arthur and me, or tried to muscle in front of each other in the cafeteria, or just happened to feel ornery on the same day. The only thing they had in common was the bad luck of getting caught by Mr. Mitchell.

Mr. Mitchell kept his eyes peeled for grudge fighters, and when he found a couple of likely candidates he signed them up on the spot. It made no difference how slight their disagreement was, or how long a time remained until the next smoker. Arthur and I were lucky; we had to wait only three weeks. There were boys in the lists who'd been waiting since September, and who would've had trouble remembering just what their grudge was supposed to be. But none of them ever refused to fight—it wasn't conceivable. They kept their enmity alive for as long as they had to, and when the time came they fought as they were expected to fight, viciously, hatefully, as if to erase one another from the earth.

Arthur and I steered clear of each other when we could, gave each other evil looks when we couldn't. It would have been indecorous and unwise for a pair of grudge fighters to let themselves get friendly. We needed to keep our hostility intact for the smoker. I had no trouble doing this. Now that the situation called for ill will, I found I had large stores of it to draw on.

We had been close. Whatever it is that makes closeness possible between people also puts them in the way of hard feelings if that closeness ends. Arthur and I were moving apart, and had been ever since we started high school. Arthur was trying to be a citizen. He stayed out of trouble and earned high grades. He played bass guitar with the Deltones, a pretty good band for which I had once tried out as drummer and been haughtily dismissed. The guys he ran around with at Concrete were all straight-arrows and strivers, what few of them there were in our class. He even had a girlfriend. And yet, knowing him as I did, I saw all this respectability as a performance, and a strained performance at that. Whatever their virtues, his new friends were dull. To fit in with them he had to hold his tongue and refrain from eccentric behavior. He had to act dull himself, which he wasn't and could only seem to be by an effort of will that was plain to me if to no one else.

The weakest part of his act was the girlfriend, Beth Mathis. Though Beth wasn't pretty she wasn't exactly a gorgon either, as you would have thought from the way Arthur treated her. He gripped Beth's hand as they walked from class to class, but he never talked to her or even looked at her. Instead he stared testily into the faces he passed as if looking for signs of skepticism or amusement. No one seemed to notice, but I did. It troubled me. It seemed so strange that I kept my mouth shut.

But I knew he was no citizen and he knew I was no outlaw—that I was not hard, or uncaring of the future, or contemptuous of opinion. I could see him knowing it as he watched me with my outlaw friends. This disbelief of his was vexing to me, as my own ill-concealed disbelief in his respectability must have been vexing to him. I could accept the distance growing between us. I wanted it there, most of the time. But I could not accept that he knew I was not the person I tried so hard to seem. For owning such knowledge there could be no pardon, for either of us, until we both pardoned ourselves for being who we were.

I did not have to draw only on my own poisons for inspiration. I had sympathizers and counselors. Some of these boys disliked Arthur, but most of them just wanted to be in on a fight without getting hit. They subjected me to endless pep talks and tutorials and demonstrations of unbeatable combinations they had devised and were willing to let me use. Dwight was in his glory. He cleared the utility room for action and put me back in training. There was no question of dry-gulching Arthur this time around. I needed a strategy. How did Arthur swing, Dwight wanted to know.

"Hard," I told him.

"Yeah, but *how?*"

Arthur and I hadn't had a real fight since that day on the road four years earlier, but we'd gone a few rounds in PE and I'd seen him spar with other boys. "Sort of like this," I said, moving my arms as Arthur did.

"So he windmills," Dwight said.

"He does it a lot faster than that," I said. "A lot harder, too."

"It doesn't matter how hard he does it. If he windmills, he's yours. He's in the bag." Dwight said that all I had to do was sidestep when Arthur came at me, then uppercut him to the jaw. It was that simple: sidestep, uppercut.

Using the peculiar patience, almost tenderness, that he reserved for instruction in combat, Dwight rehearsed this move with me several times before the smoker. I learned it but I didn't believe in it, any more than I believed in the moves I'd been shown by my other counselors. I didn't think I had a snowball's chance in hell against Arthur unless I threw strategy aside and went absolutely berserk, as he was sure to do.

EACH FIGHT CONSISTED of three one-minute rounds. All the fighters waited together in the locker room until Mr. Mitchell called them out. The locker room was dimly lit. We didn't talk. Except for the real heavies we looked almost frail in our big gloves and oversized, billowing shorts. A few boys lay back on the benches, their forearms over their eyes. The rest of us sat hunched with our gloves on our knees and stared at the floor, listening to the noise in the gym. The roar was steady, almost mechanically so, except when it fell off during the breaks between rounds and when it rose during what must have been particularly violent passages in the fight then underway. At these times the roar became almost palpable. We raised our heads, then lowered them again as the sound ebbed. Every five minutes or so the door would swing open and two more boys would go out, passing on their way the sweating, gasping wrecks whose fight had just ended.

Arthur and I had a long wait. We sat at opposite ends of the locker room and didn't look at each other. Boys came and went. I had questions about what I was doing here, and what was to come. I entered a trance of perplexity and apprehension. Then I heard my name, and jumped to my feet, and ran outside into the gym with Arthur behind me. The lights dazzled my eyes. I saw the people in the stands only as a mass of color. They roared when we ran out, and the sound was even louder than I'd thought it would be, a thrilling pagan din that washed the fear clean out of me. We went to our corners and Mr. Mitchell introduced us as two boys with bad blood between us, which, by now, we were. I raised my gloves at the sound of my name and the stands roared again. That was when I realized that I was invincible. I was going to give him a beating, the beating of his life, and I couldn't wait to start.

The bell rang and we went at it.

MY MOTHER WOULD hardly talk to me on the drive home that night, she was so appalled. She refused to understand that I'd really had to fight, that there was no choice. The entire spectacle had disgusted her, and most of all my own losing part in it. She said she'd been so mortified she had to put her face in her hands. I resented this. I thought I had run a pretty close second, and so did Dwight, who praised the use I had made of his coaching.

The truth was, I hadn't made nearly enough use of it. During the first round I followed my intention and fought like a crazy man. Arthur was all over me, his craziness proving more radical than my own. Twice his windmilling gloves came straight down on my head and knocked me to my knees. He knocked me to my knees again during the second round. After I got up he rushed me, and without calculation I sidestepped and threw him an uppercut. It stopped him cold. He just stood there, shaking his head. I hit him again and the bell rang.

I caught him with that uppercut twice more during the final round, but neither of them rocked him like that first one. That first one was a beaut. I launched it from my toes and put everything I had into it, and it shivered his timbers. I could feel it travel through him in one pure line. I could feel it hurt him. And when it landed, and my old friend's head snapped back so terribly, I felt a surge of pride and connection; connection not to him but to Dwight. I was distinctly aware of Dwight in that bellowing mass all around me. I could feel his exultation at the blow I'd struck, feel his own pride in it, see him smiling down at me with recognition, and pleasure, and something like love.

I had done well on the tests I'd taken in Seattle. But not long after my scores came in I got a rejection letter from Andover. Then St. Paul's turned me down. Then Exeter. The letters were polite, professed regret for the news they bore, and wished me well. I never heard back from Choate at all.

The rejections disappointed me, but I hadn't really counted on these schools anyway. I was counting on Deerfield. When I got their letter I went off by myself. I sat by the river and read it. I read it many times, first because I was too numb to take it all in, then to find some word or tone that would cancel out everything else the letter said, or at least give me hope for an appeal. But they knew what they were doing, the people who wrote these letters. They knew how to close the door so that no seam showed, no light glimmered at the edges. I understood that the game was over.

A week or so later the school secretary summoned me out of class to take a telephone call in the office. She said it sounded long distance. I thought it might be my brother, or even my father, but the caller turned out to be a Hill School alumnus who lived in Seattle. His name was Mr. Howard. He told me the school was "interested" in my application, and had asked him to meet with me and have a talk. Just an informal chat, he said. He said he'd always wanted to see our part of the state, and this would give him a good excuse. We arranged to meet outside Concrete High after classes let out the next day. Mr. Howard said he'd be driving a blue Thunderbird. He didn't say anything about wanting to meet my teachers, thank God.

"Whatever you do, just don't try to impress him," my mother said when I told her about the call. "Just be yourself."

WHEN MR. HOWARD asked me where we might go to talk, I suggested the Concrete drugstore. I knew there would be kids from school there. I wanted them to see me pull up in the Thunderbird and get out with this man, who was just old enough to be my father, and different from other men you might see in the Concrete drugstore. Without affecting boyishness, Mr. Howard still had the boy in him. He bounced a little as he walked. His narrow face was lively, foxlike. He looked around with a certain expectancy, as if he were ready to be interested in what he saw, and when he was interested he allowed himself to show it. He wore a suit and tie. The men who taught at the high school also wore suits and ties, but less easily. They were always pulling at their cuffs and running their fingers between their collars and their necks. To watch them was to suffocate. Mr. Howard wore his suit and tie as if he didn't know he had them on.

We sat at a booth in the back. Mr. Howard bought us milkshakes, and while we drank them he asked me about

Concrete High. I told him I enjoyed my classes, especially the more demanding ones, but that I was feeling a little restless lately. It was hard to explain.

"Oh, come on," he said. "It's easy to explain. You're bored."

I shrugged. I wasn't going to speak badly of the teachers who had written so well of me.

"You wouldn't be bored at Hill," Mr. Howard said. "I can promise you that. But you might find it difficult in other ways." He told me about his own time there in the years just before World War II. He had grown up in Seattle, where he'd done well in school. He expected that he would fall easily into life at Hill, but he hadn't. The academic work was much harder. He missed his family and hated the snowy Pennsylvania winters. And the boys at Hill were different from his friends back home, more reserved, more concerned with money and social position. He had found the school a cold place. Then, in his last year, something changed. The members of his class grew close in ways that he had never thought possible, until they were more like brothers than friends. It came, he said, from the simple fact of sharing the same life for a period of years. It made them a family. That was how he thought of the school now—as his second family.

But he'd had a rough time getting to that point, and some of the boys never got to it at all. They lived unhappily at the edge of things. These same boys might have done well if they'd stayed at home. A prep school was a world unto itself, and not the right world for everyone.

If any of this was supposed to put me off, it didn't. Of course the boys were concerned with money and social position. Of course a prep school wasn't for everyone—otherwise, what would be the point?

But I put on a thoughtful expression and said that I was aware of these problems. My father and my brother had given me similar warnings, I explained, and I was willing to endure whatever was necessary to get a good education.

Mr. Howard seemed amused by this answer, and asked me on what experience my father and brother had based their warnings. I told him that they had both gone to prep schools.

"Is that right? Where?"

"Deerfield and Choate."

"I see." He looked at me with a different quality of interest than before, as I had hoped he would. Though Mr. Howard was not a snob, I could see he was worried that I might not fit in at his school.

"My brother's at Princeton now," I added.

He asked me about my father. When I told him that my father was an aeronautical engineer, Mr. Howard perked up. It turned out he had been a pilot during the war, and was familiar with a plane my father had helped design—the P-51 Mustang. He hadn't flown it himself but he knew men who had. This led him to memories of his time in uniform, the pilots he had served with and the nutty things they used to do. "We were just a bunch of kids," he said. He spoke to me as if I were not a kid myself but someone who could understand him, someone of his world, family even. His hands were folded on the tabletop, his head bent slightly. I leaned forward to hear him better. We were really getting along. And then Huff showed up.

Huff had a peculiar voice, high and nasal. I had my back to the door but I heard him come in and settle into the booth behind ours with another boy, whose voice I did not recognize. The two of them were discussing a fight they'd seen the previous weekend. A guy from Concrete had broken a guy from Sedro Woolley's nose.

Mr. Howard stopped talking. He leaned back, blinking a little as if he had dozed off. He did not speak, nor did I. I didn't want Huff to know I was there. Huff had certain rituals of greeting that I was anxious to avoid, and if he sensed he was embarrassing me he would never let me get away. He would sink my ship but good. So I kept my head down and my mouth shut while Huff and the other boy talked about the fight, and about the girl the two boys had been fighting over. They talked about another girl. Then they talked about eating pussy. Huff took the floor on this subject, and showed no sign of giving it up. He went on at length. I heard boys hold forth like this all the time, and I did it myself, but now I thought I'd better show some horror. I frowned and shook my head, and stared down at the tabletop.

"Shall we go?" Mr. Howard asked.

I did not want to break cover but I had no choice. I got up and walked past Huff's booth, Mr. Howard behind me. Though I kept my face averted I was sure that Huff would see me, and as I moved toward the door I was waiting to hear him shout, "Hey! Dicklick!" The shout never came.

Mr. Howard drove around Concrete for a while before taking me back to school. He was curious about the cement plant, and disappointed that I could tell him nothing about what went on inside it. He was quiet for a time. Then he said, "You should know that a boys' school can be a pretty rough-and-tumble place."

I said that I could take care of myself.

"I don't mean physically rough," Mr. Howard said. "Boys talk about all kinds of things. Even at a school like Hill you don't hear a whole lot of boys sitting around at night talking about Shakespeare. They're going to talk about other things. Sex, whatever. And they're going to take the gloves off."

I said nothing.

"You can't expect everyone to be, you know, an Eagle Scout."

"I don't," I said.

"I'm just saying that life in a boys' school can come as a bit of a shock to someone who's led a sheltered life." I began to make an answer, but Mr. Howard said, "Let me just say one more thing. You're obviously doing a great job here. With your grades and so on you should be able to get into an excellent college later on. I'm not sure that a prep school is exactly the right move for you. You might end up doing yourself more harm than good. It's something to consider."

I told Mr. Howard that I had not led a sheltered life, and that I was determined to get myself a better education than the one I was getting now. In trying to keep my voice from breaking I ended up sounding angry.

"Don't misunderstand me," Mr. Howard said. "You're a fine boy and I'll be happy to give you a good report." He said these words quickly, as if reciting them. Then he added, "You have a strong case. But you should know what you're getting into." He said he would write to the school the next day, then we'd just have to wait and see. From what he understood, I was one of many boys being considered for the few remaining places.

"I assume you've got applications in at other schools," he said.

"Just Choate. But I'd rather go to Hill. Hill is my first choice."

We were parked in front of the school. Mr. Howard took a business card from his wallet and told me to call him if I had any questions. He advised me not to worry, said whatever happened would surely be for the best. Then he said good-bye and drove away. I watched the Thunderbird all the way down the hill to the main road, watched it as a man might watch a woman he'd just met leave his life, taking with her some hope of change that she had made him feel. The Thunderbird turned south at the main road and disappeared behind some trees.

I was running a board through the table saw at school and joking around with the boy next in line. Then I felt a sharp pinch and looked down. The ring finger on my left hand was spouting blood. I had cut off the last joint. It lay beside the whirling blade, fingernail and all. The boy I'd been talking to looked at it with me, his mouth working strangely, then turned and walked away. "Hey," I said. The shop was loud; no one heard. I sank to my knees. Somebody saw me and started yelling.

Horseface Greeley took me to the doctor. He brought along another teacher, who drove the car while Horseface asked me leading questions whose answers would protect him if we should ever go to court. I understood his purpose and gave him the answers he wanted. I thought that the accident had been my fault, and that it would be unfair of me to get him in trouble. I'd been a fool. I'd cut off part of my own finger. Now I wanted above all, as the only redemption left to me, to be a good sport.

The finger was a mess. My mother gave the doctor permission to take me to the hospital in Mount Vernon for surgery. I went under the knife that afternoon, and awoke the next morning with a bandage from my wrist to my remaining fingertips. I was supposed to stay in the hospital for three days, but the doctor was worried about infection and it was almost a week before I got home. By then I was addicted to morphine, which the nurses had given me freely because when I didn't get it I disturbed the ward with my screams. At first I wanted it for the pain; the pain was terrible. Then I wanted it for the peace it gave me. On morphine I didn't worry. I didn't even think. I rose out of myself and dreamed benevolent dreams, soaring like a gull in the balmy updraft.

The doctor gave me some tablets when I left the hospital, but they had no effect. I was hurting in two ways now, from my finger and from narcotic withdrawal. Though it must have been a mild episode of withdrawal it did not seem mild to me, especially since I didn't know what it was, or that it would come to an end. Knowing that everything comes to an end is a gift of experience, a consolation gift for knowing that we ourselves are coming to an end. Before we get it we live in a continuous present, and imagine the future as more of that present. Happiness is endless happiness, innocent of its own sure passing. Pain is endless pain.

If I had lived in a place where drugs were bought and sold, I would have bought them. I would have done anything to get them. But nobody I knew used drugs. The possibility didn't even occur to us. The marijuana scare films that might have sparked our interest never made it to Concrete, and heroin use was understood to be unique to the residents of New York City.

I was all through being a good sport. Everything was a grievance to me. I complained about school, I complained about the uselessness of my medicine, I complained about how hard it was to eat and dress myself. I begged for comfort and then despised it. I talked back and found fault, especially with Dwight. From behind my wound I said things to Dwight I never would have said to him before.

It occurred to me that alcohol might make me feel better. I stole some of Dwight's Old Crow but the first drink made me choke, so I replenished the bottle with water and put it back. A few nights later Dwight asked me if I had been into his whiskey. It was watery, he said. He seemed more curious than anything else. He probably would have let me off with a warning if I'd admitted it, but I said, "I'm not the drinker in this house."

"Don't talk to me like that, mister," he said, and jabbed his fingers against my chest.

He didn't push all that hard, but he caught me off balance. I stumbled backward, tripping on my own feet, and as I went down I threw my hands out behind me to break the fall. All this seemed to happen very slowly, until the moment I landed on my finger.

I forgot who I was. I heard a steady howling all around me as I thrashed on the floor. Other sounds. Then I was sitting on the couch, drenched in sweat, and my mother was trying to calm me. It was all over, she said. This was it, this was the last time. We were getting out of here.

I LEFT FIRST. After all the years of thinking about leaving, I actually did it. My mother talked to Chuck Bolger's parents and they agreed to let me live with them in Van Horn for the next few months, until the end of the school year. By then my mother hoped to have a job in Seattle. Once she started work and found a place to live I would follow her down. Mr. Bolger had serious doubts at first. He suspected that I was partly to blame for Chuck's wildness. But Chuck had been wild for years and Mr. Bolger was too smart a man not to know it, and too good a man to turn down a request for asylum. He did make certain conditions. I would help out in his store, and go to church with the rest of his family. I would accept his authority. I would neither smoke nor drink nor swear.

I gave my word on all counts.

Chuck drove up to get me. He and Pearl and my mother helped me carry my things out to the car while Dwight sat in the kitchen. When we were about to leave, Dwight came outside and watched us. I could tell he wanted to make it up with me. He already had a bad reputation in the camp, and to have one of his family leave his house like this would disgrace him. He knew I would tell people he had bullied me in my invalid condition. And though my mother had said nothing to him of her own plans to go, he must have known that with me out of the way there was nothing left to hold her, nothing but threats.

I could see him gearing up for an approach. Finally he walked over and said we ought to talk about things. I had planned to make some hurtful answer when this moment came, but all I did was shake my head and look away. I kissed my mother good-bye and told Pearl I'd see her in school.

Then I got in the car. Dwight came up to the window, and said, "Well, good luck." He put out his hand. Helpless to stop myself, I shook it and wished him good luck too. But I didn't mean it any more than he did.

We hated each other. We hated each other so much that other feelings didn't get enough light. It disfigured me. When I think of Chinook I have to search for the faces of my friends, their voices, the rooms where I was made welcome. But I can always see Dwight's face and hear his voice. I hear his voice in my own when I speak to my children in anger. They hear it too, and look at me in surprise. My youngest once said, "Don't you love me anymore?"

I left Chinook without a thought for the years I'd lived there. When we crossed the bridge out of camp, Chuck reached under his seat and brought out a jar of gorilla blood he'd mixed up for me. I worked on that while Chuck took sips from a pint of Canadian Club. I remember the wheat-colored label with the two big C's, the way Chuck squinted when he tipped the bottle, the sloshing of the liquor when he lowered it again. I remember the glint of the liquor in the corner of his mouth.

The Amen
Corner

C huck got drunk almost every night. Some nights he was jolly. Other nights he went into silent rages in which his face would redden and swell, and his lips move to the words he was shouting inside his head. At the peak of his fury he threw himself against unyielding objects. He would ram his shoulder into a wall, then back up and do it again. Sometimes he just stood there, saying nothing, and pummeled the wall with his fists. In the morning he would ask me what he'd done the night before. I didn't really believe that he had forgotten, but I played along and told him how wiped out he'd been, how totally out of control. He shook his head at the behavior of this strange other person.

I could not keep up with him and I stopped trying. He never said anything, but I knew he was disappointed in me.

Chuck's father had run a dairy before he became a store-keeper and preacher. The family still owned the farm, though now they leased the pastures and barn to a neighbor. Mr. and Mrs. Bolger and their two young daughters lived in the main house. Chuck and I were off by ourselves in a converted storage shed a couple of hundred feet away. Mr. Bolger had the idea that a good dose of trust would rouse us to some adult conception of ourselves. It should have. It didn't.

The Bolgers went to bed at nine-thirty sharp. Around ten, if Chuck wasn't already in the bag, we pushed his car down the drive a ways, then cranked it up and drove over to Veronica's house. Arch and Psycho were usually there, sometimes Huff. They drank and played poker. I had no money, so I sat on the floor and watched the late show with Veronica. Veronica ruined the movies by telling me all about the stars. She had the inside track on Hollywood. She knew which actor, supposedly dead, was actually a drooling vegetable, and which actress could not be satisfied except by entire football teams. She was especially hard on the men. According to Veronica they were all a bunch of homos, and she proved it by pointing out the little signals and gestures by which they advertised their persuasion. The lighting of a cigarette, the position of a handkerchief in a breast pocket, the way an actor glanced at his watch or angled his hat—everything was evidence to Veronica. Even when she wasn't talking I could feel her watching the men on the screen, ready to pounce.

On the way home Chuck scared me by weaving all over the road and giving sermons about damnation. He meant these sermons to be parodies of his father's, but they were all his own. Mr. Bolger did not preach like this. Chuck could catch his father's inflections and rhythms, but not his music. What came out instead was his own fear of being condemned.

I wasn't used to people who took religion seriously. My mother never had, and Dwight was an atheist of the Popular Science orthodoxy. (Jesus hadn't really died, he had taken a drug that made him look dead so he could fake a resurrection

later. The parting of the Red Sea was caused by a comet passing overhead. Manna was just the ancient word for potato.)
There was an Episcopalian minister, Father Karl, who drove
up to Chinook every couple of weeks and was entirely serious,
but the possibilities Father Karl made me feel when I listened
to him did not stay with me after he left.

Mr. Bolger was careful never to pressure me, but I understood that he was a fisher of men and that I was fair game.
Not a prize catch, maybe, but legal. The danger wasn't that he
would force me into anything but that I would force myself in
order to get on his good side. Mr. Bolger was tall and dignified.
He had a long face and brooding eyes. When I talked to him,
he looked at me in so direct a way that I sometimes forgot
what I was saying. I had the feeling that he could see into
me. He treated me with courtesy, though without affection;
always he seemed to be holding something back. I wanted
him to think well of me.

That was one danger. The other was the music. At Mr.
Bolger's church the music was passionate, not like the meno-
pausal Catholic hymns I'd learned in Salt Lake. People got
carried away singing these songs. They wept and clapped their
hands, they cried out, they swayed up the aisle to the Amen
Corner. I felt like doing it myself sometimes but I held back.
Chuck was always beside me, silent as a stone. He moved his
lips without singing. He had never been to the Amen Corner,
and I was afraid he would ridicule me if I went. So I hung
back even though I wanted, out of musical sentimentality and
eagerness to please, to go forward. And after church I was

always glad I hadn't done it, because I knew that Mr. Bolger would see through me and be disgusted.

Chuck never turned on me. In his drunkest, darkest rages he hurt only himself. That was my good luck. Chuck was bullishly built, thickset and chesty. I wouldn't have stood a chance against him. Other boys left him in peace and he left them in peace, which he was inclined to do anyway. Except with himself he was gentle—not as his father was, with that least suggestion of effort dignified men give to their gentleness, but as his mother was. He looked like her, too. Milky skin with a wintry spot of red on each cheek. Yellow hair that turned white in sunshine. Wide forehead. He also had his mother's pale blue eyes and her way of narrowing them when she listened, looking down at the floor and nodding in agreement with whatever you said.

Everyone liked Chuck. Sober, he was friendly and calm and openhanded. When I admired a sweater of his he gave it to me, and later he gave me a Buddy Holly album we used to sing along with. Chuck liked to sing when he wasn't in church. It was hard to believe, seeing him in the light of day, that he had spent the previous night throwing himself against a tree. That was why the Bolgers had so much trouble coming to terms with his wildness. They saw nothing of it. He lingered over meals in the main house, talked with his father about the store, helped his mother with the dishes. His little sisters fawned on him like spaniels. Chuck seemed for all the world a boy at home with himself, and at these times he was. It wasn't an act. So when the other Chuck, the bad

Chuck, did something, it always caught the Bolgers on their blind side and knocked them flat.

ONE NIGHT PSYCHO and Huff came over to play cards. They were as broke as I was, so I joined the game. We drank and played for matchsticks until we got bored. Then we decided that it would be a great idea to drive over to Bellingham and back. Chuck didn't have enough gas for the trip but said he knew where we could get some. He collected a couple of five-gallon cans and a length of hose, and the four of us set off across the fields.

It had rained heavily that day. A fine spray still fell through the mist around us. The ground, just ploughed for sowing, was boggy. It pulled at our shoes, then let them go with a rich mucky gasp. Psycho was wearing loafers, and he kept coming out of them. Finally he gave up and turned back. The rest of us pushed on. Every few steps we could hear Psycho shout with rage behind us.

We walked a good half mile before we got to the Welch farm. We loitered by the outbuildings for a while, then crossed the yard to Mr. Welch's truck. Chuck siphoned gas out of the tank while Huff and I watched the house. I had never been here before, but I knew the Welch boys from school. There were three of them, all sad, shabbily dressed, and quiet to the point of muteness. One of the boys, Jack, was in my class. He was forlorn and stale-smelling, like an old man who has lost his pride. Because we had the same first name it amused Mr.

Mitchell to match us up as sparring partners during PE. Then the other boys would circle us and shout, "Go, Jack! Get him, Jack! Kill him, Jack!" But Jack Welch had no stomach for it. He held his gloves up dubiously, as if he thought they might turn on him, and gave me a look of apology whenever Mr. Mitchell goaded him into taking a swing. It was strange to think of him in that dark house, his unhappy eyes closed in sleep, while I kept watch outside. Huff grunted as he scraped at his shoes with a stick. The air smelled of gasoline.

Chuck filled the cans and we started back. The going was harder than the coming. We were headed uphill now. We took turns carrying the cans, swinging them forward and stumbling after them. Their weight drove us into the mud and threw us off balance, making us flounder and fall. By the time we got back we were caked with mud. I had torn my shirt on some barbed wire. My good arm was dead from the pull of the cans, the other arm pulsing with pain where I had brushed my finger against a post. I was dead tired and so were the others. Nobody said a thing about Bellingham. While Chuck drove Huff and Psycho home, I cleaned myself off and fell into bed.

Mr. Bolger woke us late the next morning. He only put his head in the door and said, "Get up," but something in his voice snapped me upright, wide awake. Chuck too. We looked at each other and got out of bed without a word. Mr. Bolger waited by the door. Once we were dressed he said, "Come on," and set off toward the main house. He walked in long pushing strides, head bent forward as if under a weight, and never once turned to see if we were behind him. When I glanced over at Chuck his eyes were on his father's back. His face was blank.

We followed Mr. Bolger into the kitchen. Mrs. Bolger was sitting at the breakfast table, crying into a napkin. Her eyes were red and a blue vein stood out on her pale forehead. "Sit down," Mr. Bolger said. I sat down across from Mrs. Bolger and looked at the tablecloth. Mr. Bolger said that Mr. Welch had just been by, for reasons we would have no trouble figuring out. I kept quiet. So did Chuck. Mr. Bolger waited, but we still said nothing. Then, to spare himself the stupidity of a denial, he told us we'd left a trail anyone could follow. You didn't even have to follow it—you could see it all the way from here.

"How could you do such a thing?" Mrs. Bolger asked. "To the Welches, of all people?"

I looked up and saw that Mr. Bolger was studying me. We both looked away when our eyes met.

Mrs. Bolger shook with sobs. Mr. Bolger put his hand on her shoulder. "What's your excuse?" he said to Chuck.

Chuck said there wasn't any excuse.

"Jack?"

"No excuse, sir."

He looked at each of us. "Were you drinking?"

We both admitted we'd been drinking.

Mr. Bolger nodded, and I understood that this was in our favor, so great was his faith in the power of alcohol to transform a person. It also worked to our advantage that we ourselves had not suggested drink as a defense but confessed it as a further wrong. That left Mr. Bolger free to make our excuses for us.

Chuck and I were ritually abashed, Mr. Bolger ritually angry, but the worst was over and we all knew it. We spent the rest of the morning at the kitchen table, working out a plan of reparation. Chuck and I would return the gasoline, which we had been too tired to pour into his tank. We would apologize to Mr. Welch, and we would give our word not to drink again. No mention was made of the promises we had already broken. We agreed to all of Mr. Bolger's conditions but one—we would not tell him who had been with us. He harried us for their names, but it was plain to me that this was part of the ceremony, and that he was glad to find us capable at least of loyalty. Anyway, he must have known who the others were.

We stood up and shook hands. Mr. Bolger made it clear that he did not want to lord this over us. He wanted to put the whole thing behind him, the sooner the better. Mrs. Bolger did not get up. I could see that she was still feeling the wrong of what we had done, though I did not feel it myself.

CHUCK AND I loaded up the cans and drove them over to the Welch farm. It wasn't that far through the fields, but to get there by car we had to drive up to the main road and then turn off on a winding, unpaved track still muddy from yesterday's rain. Chuck went fast so we wouldn't get stuck. The mud pounded against the floor of the car. We passed through scrub pine that opened up here and there to show a house or a clearing with some cows in it. Chuck swore a blue streak the whole way.

We pulled into the Welches' drive and sat there a moment, silent, before we got out.

I had worked on several farms during my summer vacations, picking and haying. These farms were in the upper valley near Marblemount, close but not too close to the river, with good drainage and rich soil. The owners prospered. They had up-to-date equipment, and kept their houses and barns painted. Their yards were grassy, trimmed with flower beds and decorated with birdbaths and wagon wheels and big ceramic squirrels.

The Welch farmyard was all mud, a wallow without hogs. Nothing grew there. And nothing moved, no cats, no chickens, no mutts running out to challenge us. The house was small, ash gray and decrepit. Moss grew thickly on the shingle roof. There was no porch, but a tarpaulin had been stretched from one wall to give shelter to a washtub with a mangle and a clothesline that drooped with dull flannel shirts of different sizes, and dismal sheets.

Smoke rose from a stovepipe. It was surprising to look up and see that the sky was blue and fresh.

Chuck knocked. A woman opened the door and stood in the doorway, a little girl behind her. Both of them were red-haired and thin. The little girl smiled at Chuck. Chuck smiled sadly back at her.

"I was surprised," the woman said. "I have to say I was surprised."

"I'm sorry," Chuck said. He made the abashed face he'd been wearing in the kitchen that morning.

"I wouldn't have never thought it of you," she said. She looked at me, then turned back to Chuck. "You say you're sorry. Well, so am I. So is Mr. Welch. It's just not what we ever expected."

Mrs. Welch told us where to find her husband. As we slogged through the mud, the fuel cans swinging at our sides, Chuck said, "Shit, shit, shit . . ."

Mr. Welch was sitting on a pile of wood, watching Jack and one of the other Welch boys. They were a little ways off, taking turns digging with a post-holer. Mr. Welch was bareheaded. His wispy brown hair floated in the breeze. He had on a new pair of overalls, dark blue and stiff-looking and coated with mud around the ankles. We came up to him and set the cans down. He looked at them, then looked back at his sons. They kept an eye on us as they worked, not with any menace, but just to see what was going to happen. I could hear the post-holer slurping up the mud with the same sound our shoes had made the night before. Chuck waved at them and they both nodded.

We looked at them for a time. Then Chuck went to Mr. Welch's side and began to talk in a low voice, telling him how sorry he was for what we had done. He offered no explanations and did not mention that we had been drinking. His manner was weightily sincere, almost tragical.

Mr. Welch watched his sons. He did not speak. When Chuck was through, Mr. Welch turned and looked at us, and I could see from the slow and effortful way he moved that the idea of looking at us was misery to him. His cheeks were stubbled and sunken in. He had spots of mud on his face. His brown eyes were blurred, as if he'd been crying or was about to cry.

I didn't need to see the tears in Mr. Welch's eyes to know that I had brought shame on myself. I knew it when we first drove into the farmyard and I saw the place in the light of day. Everything I saw thereafter forced the knowledge in deeper. These people weren't making it. They were near the edge, and I had nudged them that much farther along. Not much, but enough to take away some of their margin. Returning the gas didn't change that. The real harm was in their knowing that someone could come upon them in this state, and pause to do them injury. It had to make them feel small and alone, knowing this—that was the harm we had done. I understood some of this and felt the rest.

The Welch farm seemed familiar to me. It wasn't just the resemblance between their house and the house where I'd lived in Seattle, it was the whole vision, the house, the mud, the stillness, the boys lifting and dropping the post-holer. I recognized it from some idea of failure that had found its perfect enactment here.

Why were Jack and his brother digging post holes? A fence there would run parallel to the one that already enclosed the farmyard. The Welches had no animals to keep in or out—a fence there could serve no purpose. Their work was pointless. Years later, while I was waiting for a boat to take me across a river, I watched two Vietnamese women methodically hitting a discarded truck tire with sticks. They did it for a good long while, and were still doing it when I crossed the river. They were part of the dream from which I recognized the Welches, my defeat-dream, my damnation-dream, with its solemn choreography of earnest useless acts.

It takes a childish or corrupt imagination to make symbols of other people. I didn't know the Welches. I had no right to see them this way. I had no right to feel fear or pity or disgust, no right to feel anything but sorry for what I had done. I did feel these things, though. A kind of panic came over me. I couldn't take a good breath. All I wanted was to get away.

Mr. Welch had said something to Chuck, something I could not hear, and Chuck had stepped aside. I understood that his apology had been accepted. Mr. Welch was waiting for mine, and the attitude of his waiting told me that this business was hard on him. It was time to get it over with. But I stayed where I was, watching the Welch boys pull up mud. I could not make myself move or speak. Just to stand there was all I could do. When Chuck realized I wasn't going to say anything, he murmured good-bye and shook Mr. Welch's hand. I followed him to the car without looking back.

MR. BOLGER KNOCKED on our door when we got home. That small courtesy was full of promise, and when he came in I saw that he was eager to be forgiving. It made me sad, being so close to his pardon and knowing I couldn't have it. He nodded at us and said, "How did it go?"

Chuck didn't answer. He had not spoken to me since we left the Welch place. I knew he despised me for not apologizing, but I had no way of explaining my feelings to him, or even to myself. I believed that there was no difference between explanations and excuses, and that excuses were unmanly. So were feelings, especially complicated feelings. I didn't admit to them. I hardly knew I had them.

Chuck surrounded himself with silence. We were close to our breaking point. I couldn't keep up with him in debauchery, and now I had failed him in repentance as well.

Mr. Bolger looked at me when he got no answer from Chuck.

"Chuck apologized," I said. "I didn't."

Mr. Bolger asked Chuck to leave us alone, and sat down on the other bed when Chuck had gone. With a show of patience, he tried to understand why I had not apologized. All I was able to say was that I couldn't.

He asked for more.

"I wanted to," I said. "I just couldn't."

"You agreed that you owed the Welches an apology."

"Yes sir."

"You promised to apologize, Jack. You gave your word."

I said again that I wanted to but couldn't.

Mr. Bolger lost interest in me then. I saw it in his eyes. He told me that he and Mrs. Bolger had hoped I would be happy with them, happier than I'd apparently been with my stepfather, but it didn't seem as if I was. All in all, he saw no point in my staying on. He said he would call my mother that night and make arrangements to have her come and get me. I didn't argue. I knew that his mind was made up.

So was mine. I had decided to join the army.

MY MOTHER DROVE down the next day. She huddled with the Bolgers for a couple of hours, then took me for a drive. At first she didn't speak. Her hands were clenched tight on the steering wheel; the muscles of her jaw were tensed. We went down the road a few miles, to a truck stop. My mother pulled into the parking lot and turned off the engine.

"I had to beg them," she said.

Then she told me what her begging had accomplished. Mr. Bolger had agreed to let me stay on after all, if I would put things right with the Welches by working on their farm after school.

I said I would rather not do that.

She ignored me. Looking over the steering wheel, she said that Mr. Bolger also wanted Father Karl to have a talk with me. Mr. Bolger hoped that Father Karl's brand of religion might reach me, being closer to the one I was raised in than his own. My mother said I had a couple of choices: I could either go along with Mr. Bolger or pack up. Today. And if I did pack up, I'd better have a plan, because I couldn't come home with her—Dwight wouldn't let me in the door. It looked like she might have a job lined up in Seattle but it would be a while until she knew for sure, and then she would need time to get started and find a place.

"Why didn't you apologize to those people?" she said.

I told her I couldn't.

She looked at me, then stared through the windshield again. She had never been so far away. If I had robbed a bank she would have stuck by me, but not for this. She said, "So what are you going to do." She didn't sound especially interested.

I told her I would do whatever the Bolgers wanted.

She started the car and took me back. After letting me out she drove away fast.

MR. BOLGER WAS too busy that week to arrange my service with the Welches, but I did not know that. I came into the store after school each day expecting to be told to go back outside and get in the car. I came in, and hesitated, and when no one said anything I walked lightly into the back room and put my apron on and began to do my chores. Chuck and I used to work together, talking, joking around, snapping dust cloths and goosing each other with broom handles. Now we worked by ourselves, in silence. I dreamed. Sometimes I thought of the Welch farm and of myself there, drowning in mud, surrounded by accusing faces. Whenever this thought came to me I had to close my eyes and catch a breath.

Toward the end of the week Father Karl came in. He talked to Mr. Bolger in the storeroom for a few minutes, then called me outside. "Let's take a walk," he said.

We followed a footpath down to the river. Father Karl didn't say anything until we were at the riverbank. He picked up a rock and threw it into the water. I had the cynical suspicion that he was going to give me the same sermon the chaplain at Scout camp had given to every new group of boys on their first day last summer. He would walk up to the edge of the lake, casually pick up a handful of stones and toss one in. "Only a pebble," he would say musingly, as if the idea were just occurring to him, "only a pebble, but look at all the ripples it makes, and how far the ripples reach . . ." By the end of the summer we camp counselors all held him in open scorn. We called him Ripples.

But Father Karl did not give this sermon. He couldn't have. He had come by his faith the hard way, and did not speak of it with art or subtlety. His parents were Jewish. They had both been killed in concentration camps, and Father Karl himself barely survived. Sometime after the war he became a convert to Christianity, and then a minister. Some trace of Eastern Europe still clung to his speech. He had dark good looks of which he seemed unaware, and a thoughtful manner that grew sharp when he had to deal with pretense or frivolity. I had felt this sharpness before, and was about to feel it again.

He asked me who I thought I was.

I did not know how to answer this question. I didn't even try.

"Look at yourself, Jack. What are you doing? Tell me what you think you are doing."

"I guess I'm screwing up," I said, giving my head a rueful shake.

"No baloney!" he shouted. "No baloney!"

He looked about ready to hit me. I decided to keep quiet.

"If you go on like this," he said, "what will happen to you? Answer me!"

"I don't know."

"Yes you do. You know." His voice was softer. "You know." He picked up another rock and hurled it into the river. "What do you want?"

"Sorry?"

"Want! You must *want* something. What do you want?"

I knew the answer to this question, all right. But I was sure that my answer would enrage him even more, worldly as I knew it to be, and contrary to what I could imagine of his own wants. I could not imagine Father Karl wanting money, a certain array of merchandise, wanting, at any price, the world's esteem. I could not imagine him wanting anything as much as I wanted these things, or imagine him hearing my wants without contempt.

I had no words for any of this, or for my understanding that to accept Father Karl's hope of redemption I would have to give up my own. He believed in God, and I believed in the world.

I shrugged off his question. I wasn't exactly sure what I wanted, I said.

He sat down on a log. I hesitated, then sat a little ways down from him and stared across the river. He picked up a stick and prodded the ground with it, then asked me if I wanted to make my mother unhappy.

I said no.

"You don't?"

I shook my head.

"Well, that's what you're doing."

I said nothing.

"All right, then. Do you want to make her happy?"

"Sure."

"Good. That's something. That's one thing you want. Right?" When I agreed, he said, "But you're making her unhappy, aren't you?"

"I guess."

"No guessing to it, Jack. You are." He looked over at me. "So why don't you stop? Why don't you just stop?"

I didn't answer right away, for fear of seeming merely agreeable. I wanted to appear to give his question some serious thought. "All right," I said. "I'll try."

He threw down the stick. He was still watching me, and I knew that he understood what had happened here; that he had not "reached me" at all, because I was not available to be reached. I was in hiding. I had left a dummy in my place to look sorry and make promises, but I was nowhere in the neighborhood and Father Karl knew it.

Still, we didn't leave right away. We sat gazing out across the water. The river was swollen with runoff. More brown than green, it chuckled and hissed along the bank. Farther from shore it seethed among mossy boulders and the snarled roots of trees caught between them. From under the changing surface sounds of the river came a deep steady sigh that never changed, and grew louder as you listened to it until it was the only sound you heard. Birds skimmed the water. New leaves glinted on the aspens along the bank.

It was spring. We were both caught in it for a moment, forgetful of our separate designs. We were with each other the way kindred animals are with each other. Then we stirred, and remembered ourselves. Father Karl delivered some final admonition, and I said I would do better, and we walked back to the store.

That weekend Mr. Bolger told me that he had spoken to the Welches and that they had refused my help. "They wouldn't have you," he said, and let me know by the gravity of his expression that this was the ultimate punishment, a punishment far worse than doing hard time on their farm. He actually succeeded in making me feel disappointed. But I got over it.

The sheriff came to the house one night and told the Bolgers that Chuck was about to be charged with statutory rape. Huff and Psycho were also named in the complaint. The girl was in my class at Concrete High—one of a pack of hysterically miserable girls who ran around in tight clothes, plastered their faces with makeup, chainsmoked and talked in class and did their best to catch the attention of boys who would be sure to use them badly. Somebody had knocked her up. She'd kept her pregnancy secret for as long as she could, and she was so fat to begin with that this deception came within two months of bringing her to term. Her name was Tina Flood, but everyone just called her The Flood. She was fifteen years old.

The sheriff had talked to Tina, and on the basis of what she said he'd persuaded her father to hold off awhile before filing charges. Tina had said she didn't want to charge anyone with anything, she just wanted Chuck to marry her. Mr. Flood, on the other hand, wanted to send the whole bunch of them to jail. But he must have known that this would do nothing for his daughter, and he must also have known that for Tina to marry into a family like the Bolgers would be a piece of luck wilder than anyone could have sanely imagined for her.

So he had taken the sheriff's advice. He was just waiting for Chuck to say the word.

Chuck came back from the house that night and sat on his bed and told me everything. He also told me that he had no intention of marrying Tina Flood. He'd said this to the sheriff, too, said he'd spend the rest of his life in jail first. The sheriff told him not to make up his mind too fast. He would keep Mr. Flood at bay until Chuck had a chance to think about it and talk things over with his folks. But he left no doubt of the outcome if Chuck turned Tina down. He would go to prison. The charge was serious, and the case against him and the others was rock solid.

Chuck said he wouldn't do it.

I told him I wouldn't either. I encouraged him, but in my heart I was glad he was in trouble, and not just because it would take the heat off me. I was still hurt that he had deserted me in my own trouble. It did not displease me to see Chuck on the griddle now, and to have the chance to show him that I was a better friend than he had been. I would stand up for him.

No one else did. Not Huff or Psycho, not even his parents. Mrs. Bolger was in too much pain even to speak to him. She wept constantly, and hardly ever left the house. Mr. Bolger's worry for her expressed itself in implacable anger toward Chuck. He rode Chuck hard, and when he wasn't riding him he watched him furiously, especially during meals. Dinner was the worst time of the day. No one spoke. The sounds of steel on china, of chewing and swallowing, of chairs creaking, all seemed amplified and grotesque. Chuck's sisters bolted their food and got out of there. So did I. Chuck had to stay, and then, when everyone else was gone, get browbeaten by his father.

Mr. Bolger wanted him to marry Tina Flood. Chuck had lain with the girl, as he himself admitted. It made no difference whether she had also been with two other boys or a hundred, Chuck had lain with her and by that act he had become responsible for what might happen to her afterward. He had no right to refuse the responsibility just because it was hard. He had played at being a man; now the time had come to be a man.

Mr. Bolger must have gagged on his own counsel. He was generous but proud, too proud to utter without mortification these arguments designed to win him The Flood for a daughter-in-law. But he accepted the cost of his principles and kept his feelings to himself.

Huff and Psycho also wanted Chuck to marry Tina, but their reasons were simpler than Mr. Bolger's. If he didn't marry her, they would both go to Walla Walla with him. This seemed unnecessary and unfair. All Chuck had to do was bite the bullet for a few years and then dump her.

Chuck wouldn't do that. He did not explain his reasons to Huff and Psycho, or even to his father, but at night, when he felt most embattled and alone, he explained them to me. He had to work at putting them into words, and always seemed a little surprised to hear them. So was I. Basically, Chuck would not marry Tina Flood because he believed himself to be otherwise engaged. Sure, he liked to fool around, but way down deep he was saving himself for his wife. He had a clear picture of her, and when he finally met her he was going to marry her and stay married forever. The wife for whom Chuck was saving himself was a television wife, cute, sassy, and pious. Their life together would be a heartwarming series with lots of affectionate banter. It would also have some religious content; the husband Chuck was saving for his wife was a man just dying to see the error of his ways, and to mend them. To put liquor, gambling, and fornication behind him forever, along with the bad companions of his reckless youth. Once married, children, and plenty of them. Sobriety. Fidelity. Grace at dinner and a full pew on Sundays.

He wanted a good life. The good life he had in mind for himself was just as conventional as the one I had in mind for myself, though without its epic pretensions. And Chuck still had faith in his, whereas I was losing mine. I didn't have a clue what was going to happen to me. My life was a mess, and because I understood the problem as one of bad luck I could imagine no remedy but good luck, which I didn't seem to have.

Chuck held on to his dream as if it were already actual. He was even prepared to go to prison for it. Tina Flood and the baby she carried were not real to him. They were just another entry in the ledger of past mistakes which would give drama to his future change of heart, and which the virtue of his married life would atone for.

The sheriff had expected Chuck to back down after a few days. When this didn't happen he started talking tough. Mr.

Flood wouldn't wait any longer, he said. The charges were going to be filed any day now, and once the case went to court Chuck would have no chance of probation. The sheriff wanted Chuck to understand that he wasn't bluffing about this. A boy and a girl was one thing, but three men and a girl was something else. In the eyes of the law Chuck and his friends were men, and they would be punished as men.

Chuck did not give in. The idea of going to prison scared him, but he refused to consider marrying Tina Flood. Even the suggestion made him sick. He came back from brow-beating sessions at the house with his eyes burning and a feverish sheen of sweat on his face. My own idea was that he should run off and join the army, but he wouldn't give this any thought. He was frozen in the path of the future rush-ing down on him, with only enough strength left to say no to poor Tina Flood.

When he started crying in his bed at night, I lost my secret pleasure in his situation. I wanted to do for him what I used to do for my mother, throw an arm around him and speak some words of comfort. But that wasn't possible between us, and anyway I could tell he was trying not to be heard.

IN THE MIDDLE of all this I had another telephone call at school from Mr. Howard. He was shouting on the other end of the line as if we had a bad connection, which we did not. He told me that I'd been awarded a scholarship to the Hill School. He had spoken to the director of admissions just that morning. I would be getting an official letter in a couple of days, but he wanted to let me know in person and to tell me how happy he was for me. And he was happy. I could hear it in his voice, as if it were some good news of his own he had called to tell me about.

He said he'd been pretty sure I'd get it, as sure as one could be about these things. But he had thought it best not to raise my hopes too high. Anything could have happened. "Still," he said, "I would've been very surprised if you hadn't gotten it, after the letter I wrote."

Mr. Howard said we had a lot to talk about. He wanted to tell me more about life at Hill, so I wouldn't be completely unprepared for what I found. There was also the problem of clothes. I would need an extensive wardrobe just to meet the school's basic requirements. These clothes really had to be of a certain cut and quality. He wished he could say that boys at Hill didn't care about such things, but unfortunately they did, like boys anywhere else. Mr. Howard did not want me to feel out of place. What he proposed to do, if my mother agreed, was take me to his own tailor in Seattle and set me up with everything I might need. He wanted me to tell my mother that he would consider it a favor if she would allow him to do this.

He would call back to arrange details. "I'm very happy for you," he said again. I had hardly spoken at all. After Mr. Howard hung up I went back to my algebra class, which I was failing, and watched the teacher's mouth move for the rest of the period.

* * *

THE LETTER CAME. I had received a scholarship of $2,300 a year against the annual fee of $2,800. The director of admissions congratulated me on my school record and test scores, and said that the headmaster joined him in welcoming me to their community. Unfortunately, because so few of my courses at Concrete had been academic, I did not have enough credits to enter Hill as a fifth former, or junior. They had enrolled me in the fourth form instead. I shouldn't worry about this, he told me. It was common practice to hold back students coming from the more vocational public schools. There would be other boys in the same position, and the extra year would help me settle in at Hill and establish a strong record before applying to college.

The director of admissions sent me warm regards and passed on those of the headmaster. They both looked forward to meeting me in September.

I read the letter obsessively, trying out words like *headmaster* and *fourth form*. The director of admissions had enclosed an alumni bulletin filled with pictures of Gothic-style buildings on emerald lawns, big trees in autumn color, playing fields, and the boys themselves in various attitudes of work and worship and athletic striving. Here were more words to taste. *Lacrosse. Squash. Glee Club.* The students looked different from the boys I knew. It wasn't just a difference of clothes and hairstyle. The difference was tribal—bones, carriage, a signature set of expressions. I pondered these pictures the way I pondered pictures of Laplanders and Kurds in *National Geographic*. Some faces were closed to me. I could not feel the boys behind them. In others I sensed a generous, unguarded spirit. I studied each of them closely, wondering who he was and whether he would become a friend of mine.

There were class notes in the back of the bulletin.

"R.T. 'Chip' Bladeswell, '52, recently heard the chimes at midnight with old relay partner R. Houghton 'Howdy' Emerson IV and his wife 'Noddy' (Miss Porter's, '55). Howdy and Noddy have set up housekeeping in the Windy City while Howdy thinks up ways to help Armour out-swift Swift. Seems Chip had 'business' in Oak Park the next day with one Miss Sissy Showalter-Price (Madeira, '55). They plan to tie the knot in June. Ever since the announcement appeared, residents of Greenwich have reported widespread sounds of wailing and gnashing teeth. Hmmm . . . wunda who *dat* c'd be? Nuff said. Good luck, Sissy! (Hint: When last seen, Chip was handing off to Howdy on the corner of East Wacker and Lakeshore Drive, with Noddy in hot pursuit . . .)

"R. S. K. Unsworth St. John, '46, was recently named Director of Marketing Research for Newcombe Industries. Well done, Un!"

There were several pages of these notes, some of them accompanied by pictures of smiling, confident men in business suits, tennis whites, golf outfits. The last page of the bulletin had nothing but pictures of babies—all boys, all sons of alumni, and all of them wearing little white sweaters with a big H on the breast. The classes of 1978 and 1979 were already starting to fill up.

The director of admissions had sent me a form to complete, a straightforward information sheet. I did not send this back right away. I carried it around with me for a few days, then filled it out. Where it asked me for my name as I wished it to appear in the school catalogue, I wrote, "Tobias Jonathan von Ansell-Wolff III."

MY MOTHER PICKED me up after school one afternoon and took me into Concrete for a Coke. She couldn't get over the fact that I had been given a scholarship to Hill. She kept looking at me curiously, then laughing. "All right," she said. "What did you tell them?"

"What do you mean, what did I tell them. I didn't tell them anything. I just applied."

"Come on."

"My test scores were pretty high."

"You must have told them something."

"Thanks, Mom. Thanks for the vote of confidence."

"Are you going to get in trouble?"

"*Get in trouble.* What's that supposed to mean?"

"Are you going to get in trouble?"

"No. I'm not going to get in trouble."

"Promise?"

"I'm not going to get in trouble, *I promise.* What do you want, blood?"

We passed on to other things. She was happy for me, after all, and willing not to question fortune too closely.

She had good news of her own. She'd found a job in Seattle, a secretarial job at Aetna Life Insurance. She was supposed to start there in another week. A woman she knew had offered to put her up until she found a place to live so she wouldn't be under pressure to rent something she didn't like. She could afford to relax and take her time, especially since I would be going off to California in June rather than coming to live with her. My father had been in touch, she told me. He'd arranged everything. I would take the bus down to La Jolla as soon as school let out, and Geoffrey would join me there after his graduation from Princeton.

"What about you?" I said.

"What about me?"

"Are you going to come too? Later, if things go all right?"

"I'd be a fool if I did," she said morosely, as if she knew that wouldn't keep her from doing it.

We talked about Dwight and his little ways. How he used to stay up late counting all the pieces of candy in the house to see how many I'd eaten that day. How he used to run into the living room when he came home and put his hand on top of the TV to see if it was warm. How he bought vacuum cleaner bags by the dozen and wrote month-apart dates on each one so they would last exactly a year. My mother said he'd been on his best behavior since she started looking for work. He didn't want her to leave. Now that she'd found a job he was falling all over himself to be nice to her. He was sort of courting her, she said. Being friendly and having Pearl cozy up to her all the time. He had even applied for a transfer to Seattle so he could be close to her.

"I don't get it," she said. "He doesn't even like me. He just wants to hang on. It's so strange."

Then my mother said she had something to tell me, and I knew from the way she said it that it wasn't going to be good. It was about my money, she said, the money Dwight had been saving for me from my paper route. She knew I was planning to use it to pay the fees not covered by my scholarship. The trouble was, Dwight hadn't really been saving it. It wasn't there. Not a penny of it. She had asked him about it and he stalled and avoided the subject until she finally cornered him, and then he admitted that he didn't have it. He also didn't have the money she had earned at the cookhouse. The account was completely empty.

"I'll get the five hundred," she said, "don't worry about that."

All I could do was look at her.

"There isn't anything we can do about it. It's gone. You just have to forget about it."

That wasn't what I was doing. I wasn't forgetting about it. I was remembering it. Over $1,300. But it wasn't really the money that made me feel sorry for myself, it was the time. For two and a half years I had spent all my afternoons delivering papers. Most nights I went out again after dinner to collect from my subscribers and to try to recruit new ones. People didn't like to pay me. Even the honest ones put me off again and again. Then there were the deadbeats. They either told me sob stories about lost checks and doctor bills or turned off the lights and the TV when they heard me coming, then whispered and peered out the blinds until I gave up and left. In the winter my shoes were always wet and my head stuffed up, my nose chapped and red. I was bored crazy. One of my ways of distracting myself was to tally up over and over again, to the last penny, the money I had made.

I said, "What happened to it?"

My mother shrugged and said, "Beats me." She was ready for a change of subject. Her tolerance was good for most things, but she had no time for crybabies. Whining turned her to ice.

I didn't stop. "That was my money," I said.

"I know," she said.

"He stole it."

"He probably meant to pay you back. I don't know. It's gone. I don't know what I'm supposed to do about that. I said I'd pay the school bills."

I pulled a face.

"It's probably a little my fault too." She said she should have known better than to let Dwight handle the money, she should have insisted on a joint account. But it was a point of pride with him to deal with the finances and she hadn't wanted to get him all worked up over it. She'd wanted all of us to get along.

We finished our Cokes and walked up the street to the car, my mother moving with the buoyancy of someone who has just dropped a burden. When she was worried she wore a pale, tight-lipped mask. Lately it had started to become her own face. Now the mask was gone. She looked young and pretty. The day was warm, the air hazy with cement dust. Logging trucks banged past us through the town, grinding gears and spewing black exhaust. As we walked we made plans. Considered different possibilities. We were ourselves again—restless, scheming, poised for flight.

CHUCK CONGRATULATED ME when I told him about the scholarship, but I was careful not to let my happiness show too much. His day of reckoning was at hand and he might well have wondered why we should have drawn such different cards. This question would have crossed my mind if I had been in his place. But he probably thought nothing of the kind. He didn't want what I wanted, and he was a lot more interested in what was going to become of himself than in what was going to become of me.

Then the sheriff paid his last visit. He hadn't dropped by in over a week, and he had left that night in an angry mood, fed up with Chuck's bullheadedness. He'd given Chuck an ultimatum: Get with the program or else. If Chuck did not call him with the answer he wanted by such and such a day, he was going to let justice take its course. Chuck hadn't called the sheriff with the answer he wanted. He hadn't called him at all.

We heard his cruiser in the drive. The sound of the big engine was familiar to us by now. Chuck put his shoes on and waited for Mr. Bolger to come and get him, then the two of them walked up to the house. While he was gone I kept going to the window and looking out. I had a bad feeling through and through.

When Chuck came back I was sitting on my bed in a kind of trance. He looked at me without any sign of recognition and closed the door gently behind him. Then he jumped on the floor and started pounding it with his fists like a brat having a tantrum, except that instead of crying he was laughing. After he'd done this a while he got up and staggered from wall to wall. His face was red. He grabbed me by the shoulders and danced me across the room. "Wolfman!" he shouted. "Wolfman!"

"Yo, Chuckles."

"I love you, Wolfman! I fucking love you!"

I said "Terrific," but I was watching him.

"Listen, Wolfman. Listen." He leaned into my face. "There's gonna be a wedding, Wolfman. The old wedding bells are gonna chime. What do you think of that?"

"I don't know," I said. "What do you think?"

"What do I think? I think it's fucking great, Wolfman, what do you fucking think I think?" He went into the closet and got his Canadian Club. "Let's drink to the bride," he said. He took a drink and handed me the bottle. "Now drink to the lucky groom," he said. "Go on, drink up." He grabbed the bottle back and said, "What are you gonna call Tina after the wedding, Wolfman?"

I didn't know what to say.

"What are you gonna call her?"

I told him I didn't know.

"How about Mrs. Huff?" he said. "How about Mrs. Gerald Lucius Huff?" When he saw how I looked at him, he held up his right hand and said, "Gospel, Wolfman. I shit you not."

"Huff? Huff's marrying Tina?"

Chuck started to answer but suddenly bent over, coughing and snorting. Canadian Club ran out of his nose. I pounded him on the back. I heard myself cawing harshly. Something was breaking loose in me, some hysterical heartless tide of joy. I could hardly breathe. My face twitched. I was shaking with relief and joy and cruel pleasure, for the truth was I didn't like Huff and felt no pity for Tina. To me she was just The Flood and now I saw Huff trapped in its grip, paddling feebly on its broad heaving surface, pummeled and smothered, going under and bobbing up again somewhere else with his hairy arms churning and his pompadour agleam.

Pearl felt abandoned after my mother left, and I was sorry for her. I let her eat lunch with me sometimes. We had, after all, plenty to talk about. I patronized her shamelessly and she let me do it, listening without argument to my frank opinions on the measures she should take to make herself cuter and more popular. In fact she wasn't so bad, especially since my mother had taken her to a doctor to have her bald spot fixed. She had a gaunt sinewy beauty, but I didn't see it. I thought she was pathetic and so did she.

On a warm Friday afternoon in May we carried our lunches to the bleachers overlooking the football field. Other kids were eating and smoking in bunches around us, staring out at the brilliant grass as if a game were in progress. We talked about one thing and another, and Pearl mentioned that Dwight was planning to drive down to Seattle that night, supposedly to spend the weekend with Norma but really to see my mother and try to talk her into getting back together. He was bringing Pearl along for extra ammunition.

I didn't like hearing this. Chuck would be driving me down to Seattle the next day so I could have lunch with Mr. Howard and get fitted for my clothes, and I had hoped to go see my mother on the way home. Now that there was a chance of running into Dwight I had to give the idea up.

But later that day I saw exactly what to do. Chuck agreed to help, though with certain conditions. An hour or so past midnight we pushed his car out to the main road, then drove up the valley to Chinook. Chuck kept to the speed limit and did not drink.

The camp was dark and silent. When we got close to the house, Chuck turned off the lights and cut the engine and coasted to a stop. Dwight's Ford was nowhere in sight. I got out and looked around back, just to be sure. Chuck stayed in the car. We both believed that as long as he did not enter the house or touch anything he could not be held legally responsible if I got caught.

The door was unlocked, as always. I put on the gloves I had brought along and let myself into the utility room. I knew I should tend to business and get out of there fast, but instead I wandered into the kitchen. The refrigerator was almost empty. I put together a peanut butter sandwich and poured myself a glass of milk and carried them in my gloved hands from one room to the next, flipping on light switches until the house was ablaze.

Pearl's room smelled of perfume. I sat at her desk and read her diary. She hadn't written in it since the last time I looked. I got up and went down the hall to my old room. Both beds were bare. Skipper still had a few things around, old boots, fishing gear, a stack of car magazines, but my Scout uniform hanging in the closet was the only sign that I had ever lived there.

I went to Dwight's room. Even though I knew he was gone I held my breath and turned the doorknob slowly, then threw the door open. The bed was unmade. The air smelled sour. I turned on the light and poked around. In one of the dresser drawers I found a carton of Camels from which I shook two packs. I also found a stack of official Scout forms, including those that Scoutmasters sent to headquarters to report their boys' completion of the requirements for various ranks and badges. I took a few of these. If Dwight wouldn't promote me to Eagle, I'd just have to promote myself.

I went to the kitchen, rinsed out the glass, put it back in the cupboard. Then I turned off all the lights in the house and carried a couple of target rifles out to the car. Chuck came around to open the trunk and started hissing at me. What the fuck was I doing, where the fuck had I been? I could see he was beside himself, so I didn't try to answer. I went back in the house and got the two shotguns. Then I got the Marlin and the Garand. On my last trip I rounded up the Zeiss binoculars and the Puma hunting knife and a tooled leather scabbard Dwight had bought for the Marlin. He'd planned to use it when he went elk hunting by horseback, something he had never gotten around to doing.

Chuck arranged these things in the trunk and covered them with the sandbags he carried for traction when it snowed. Then we cleared out. Chuck was still browned off at me, but too rattled to say anything. He kept to the speed limit again and drove with histrionic correctness. Our big fear was getting stopped. The possibility made us edgy and silent.

301

We smoked. We listened to the radio, the songs blaring and fading as mountain gave way to field and field to mountain. We looked out the window at the looming purple shapes of the mountains, at the river, at the deserted winding road. Whenever we met another car Chuck reflexively dimmed the lights and slowed down as if he'd been speeding. He drove so fussily that any competent patrolman would have pulled us over on the spot.

But we were lucky. We made it home, pushed the car down the drive, went to bed and caught ourselves a few hours sleep before Mr. Bolger had one of the girls come down to fetch us for breakfast. Mr. Bolger was in good humor. He had reason to be. The morning was fresh, Chuck was still free and single, and in another couple of weeks I would be on my way to California. While we feasted on ham and grits and eggs, Mr. Bolger spread a map on the table and marked our route to Seattle. Without actually saying so, he gave us to understand that this trip was a new chance to prove ourselves. We were to drive directly to Seattle and directly home. No sidetrips. No hitchhikers. No drinking. Mr. Bolger tried to be stern as he gave us our marching orders, but it was clear that he enjoyed sending us off on what he considered to be a business of some pith and moment, which it was, if not exactly in the way he imagined.

I met Mr. Howard at Ivar's Acres of Clams down on the wharf. His wife was with him, a tall fine-boned woman with black hair just beginning to gray—a few strands that made the rest of her hair seem even blacker. She had deep-set, watchful dark eyes. Even when she smiled I felt her taking my measure, felt the force of her curiosity. It wasn't an arrogant curiosity: she wanted to know who I was. To be looked at that way is unsettling when you feel in danger of being seen through and exposed. I kept my eyes on Mr. Howard, who, under the pretext of warning me about the pitfalls of life at Hill, was happily reminiscing about his own years there—the friends he'd had and the stunts they'd pulled, like flooding the dormitory floor with water, opening the windows so it would freeze, then playing hockey through the rooms. I could see that he considered some of his memories too hot to handle. He would smile at them, then shake his head and pass on to something else. His speech turned peppery. A silly grin stole over his face. He seemed to get younger and younger, as if talking about being a boy had changed him into one.

Mrs. Howard relaxed her scrutiny. When I got lost in the menu she helped me decide what to order. We talked about *Julius Caesar*, which I was reading in English, and she mentioned that she did fund-raising for the Seattle Repertory Theater.

She was a damned fine actress in her own right, Mr. Howard said.

She made a face.

"Well, it's true," he said. I could see that he admired her and expected me to admire her too. There was an air of partnership about them that I felt warmed by.

We were sitting in a corner table overlooking the water. Gulls strutted on the railing outside, shaking their feathers and turning their heads at us. The air was rich with the smell of chowder. Sunlight gleamed on the silver, lit up the ice cubes in our glasses, made the tablecloth bright as a snowfield. I was lazily content, like the Old Pioneer whose verses covered our placemats:

No longer a slave of Ambition
I laugh at the World and its shams,
As I think of my happy condition
Surrounded by acres of clams!

Mr. Howard was quiet during lunch. He ate half his food in silence, then pushed the rest around his plate. He asked me a couple of polite questions and paid no attention to the answers. Then, with an affectation of nonchalance that put me on guard, he said there was something we needed to talk about. Something serious.

I felt myself die a little.

He hemmed and hawed awhile, then he asked if by any chance I'd had second thoughts about going off to Hill. It wasn't too late to change my mind, he said. The big thing was, I shouldn't be afraid of disappointing him or letting him down in any way. He was worried that he might have been too much of a booster, might have pushed me toward a decision I really ought to come to on my own. After all, this would be one heck of a big move, and if I didn't want to make it then I shouldn't. I was doing a terrific job up there in Concrete, a bang-up job. Going to Hill was a bit of a gamble. I might not like it. I might even do badly there, which would leave me worse off than I was now. This was a possibility that had to be taken into account.

He sat back. Well, what did I think?

I looked at him. He actually wanted an answer. I told him I'd given the question serious thought and decided to go.

"What about your mother?" Mrs. Howard said. "I imagine this is going to be hard on her, the two of you being separated after all these years."

I allowed that it would be hard on her—very hard. But we'd talked about it quite a lot, I said, and my mother was resigned to my going. In fact she was in favor of it. You could even say she was dead set on it.

"That's generous of her," Mrs. Howard said. "I hope I'll be as generous when the time comes."

She and Mr. Howard looked at each other.

After a moment he said, "So. Your mind's made up?"

"Yes sir."

He said "Great!" and smacked his hands together, and I could see that any other answer would have broken his heart.

THERE WERE THREE men folding clothes in the back of the tailor shop when we came in. One of them walked over to us, a gray-skinned man with an Adam's apple as big as a goiter. I had to force myself not to stare at it. Mr. Howard introduced him to me as Franz and me to him, without evident irony, as Mister Wolff. Franz inclined his head but did not offer to shake hands with me, nor did he speak. His eyes were milky. While Mr. Howard told Franz what we needed, Mrs. Howard sat down in one of a group of red leather chairs arranged around a frayed Oriental rug. Two white-haired men in dark suits were already seated there, both of them smoking cigars and dropping the ashes into columnar brass ashtrays filled with sand. The shop was panelled in dark wood. Fox-hunting prints hung between the tall mirrors. The plank floor was lustrous and covered with scraps of material and thread.

One of the men said something to Mrs. Howard and she said something back. Then he looked at me. His nose was purple and bulbous. "Off to Hill, are you?" he said.

"Yes sir."

"I used to wrestle against you fellows. Powerful team, Hill. A veritable juggernaut." That was all he said. A few moments later he and the other man doused their cigars and left the shop.

Mr. Howard led me to a mirror and Franz followed with an armful of jackets. Mr. Howard flipped through them until he found one that interested him. He had me put it on, then stood behind me and squinted at my reflection.

"Do you have this in a darker tweed?"

"Yesss," Franz said heavily.

"Let's see it."

Franz brought another jacket. Mr. Howard made me turn this way and that, button the jacket, unbutton it. "The sleeves are long," he said.

Franz measured the sleeves and made a notation in the ledger he carried.

Mr. Howard sent me to the changing room to try on a suit, then again to try on another one. Franz took the measurements and pinned the cuffs but he registered no opinions, not even with the subtlest change of expression. He stood quietly by as Mr. Howard rummaged through the heaps of clothes he brought, tossing ten things aside for every one he so much as paused to look at again or run between his fingers. Mr. Howard flung the rejects away with a peremptory gesture. His eyes were narrowed, his cheeks flushed. Mrs. Howard watched him with a look of amusement and pride.

I was worried that he wouldn't find anything he liked, but kept my mouth shut. I understood that I was being outfitted not for pleasure but for survival, that these clothes were a finely nuanced language that the boys in my new world would read at a glance and judge me by, even as I had judged other boys by the uniforms they wore.

I kept quiet and did as I was told. Mr. Howard sent me back and forth between the changing room and the mirror. While Franz stood waiting with his pins and tape measure Mr. Howard adjusted the length of a pant leg, raising and lowering it until it fell just so on the shoe. He tugged at my sleeves and turned me around and squared my shoulders as if he were sculpting me. If he was satisfied with something he nodded at Franz, and Franz put it aside. A pile grew. Two jackets, one of Donegal, the other of Harris tweed. A blazer. A suit. Several pairs of pants in gabardine and twill. A dozen Oxford shirts. Ties. A raincoat. Corduroy pants and flannel shirts for "hacking around," as Mr. Howard put it. A pair of Weejuns, a pair of dress shoes, and a pair of brogans—also for hacking around. Three sweaters. Then another pile of clothes for warm weather, and another for sports. It was decided that I should return to the shop in two weeks for a final fitting. Mr. Howard would collect the clothes when they were done and ship them to Hill in August so they'd be waiting for me when I got there.

I still needed a dark suit for Sundays. Mr. Howard had me try on four or five, barely distinguishable to me, before he found one worth considering. He knelt beside me and set the length of the pant legs. Then he straightened up and inspected my reflection, prodding me and turning me around as he did so. By now I was limp as dough. Mr. Howard moved behind me. He knotted a tie around my neck and stood there, hands on my shoulders, looking pensively at the mirror.

"He's going to need an overcoat," Mrs. Howard said.

"Right!" Mr. Howard said. "An overcoat. I knew there was something else."

Franz walked over to a rack and took down some overcoats for Mr. Howard to look at. He went straight to a black one with a fine herringbone weave. "Try this," he told me. I took it. It was silky to the touch, like cat's fur. "Wait," Mrs. Howard said when I began to put it on. She came over and held out her hands for the coat. With a feeling of bitterness I surrendered it. "Mmm," she said. "Cashmere." She turned me toward the mirror and settled the coat on my shoulders like a cape. She looked me up and down. She didn't say anything for a moment. Then she said, "A scarf."

"Something in navy," Mr. Howard said.

She shook her head. "He'd look like an undertaker. Claret."

Franz gave her a choice of three scarves. She moved her hand over them, wiggling her fingers like someone deciding on a chocolate, then picked one up and draped it around my neck. It had the same silky texture as the overcoat. Mrs. Howard arranged the scarf so it hung casually between the lapels of the overcoat. She glanced at me again and then stepped back so that I was alone before the mirror. The elegant stranger in the glass regarded me with a doubtful, almost haunted expression. Now that he had been called into existence, he seemed to be looking for some sign of what lay in store for him.

He studied me as if I held the answer.

Luckily for him, he was no judge of men. If he had seen the fissures in my character he might have known what he was in for. He might have known that he was headed for all kinds of trouble, and, knowing this, he might have lost heart before the game even got started.

But he saw nothing to alarm him. He took a step forward, stuck his hands in his pockets, threw back his shoulders and cocked his head. There was a dash of swagger in his pose, something of the stage cavalier, but his smile was friendly and hopeful.

Chuck had spent the afternoon at a double feature. I met him outside the theater and we drove over to Pioneer Square. I had kept him waiting for more than an an hour, and he was worried about the business still ahead of us, so he didn't say much. I could tell he was at the end of his rope where I was concerned. His mouth was set in a line. He lit one cigarette off another. He drove with dowdy rectitude, now and then sighing heavily.

I went into three pawnshops before I found anyone who would give me the time of day. The third shop was run by a woman. She was as tall as I was, and had the stiff blond hair, spiky eyelashes, and smooth, waxy face of a doll. When I said I had some things to sell she busied herself with the merchandise on the back shelf. Her hands were red and big and covered with turquoise jewelry. She didn't look at me, not then or at any other time while I was in her shop.

What kinds of things, she wanted to know. Her voice was low and flat.

Four rifles, I told her. Also two shotguns. A couple of other items.

"Where'd you get them?"

"My father left them to me," I said. "After he died." When she didn't say anything, I added, "My mom needs the money."

She grunted. This was the moment when the other pawnbrokers had told me to get lost. "Get your thieving ass out of here," was what the first one had said.

I watched her pick things up and set them down again, record players, clarinets, toasters, cameras, whatever came to hand. The shop was long and narrow. Electric guitars hung from the ceiling. Rifles and shotguns were locked in racks against the far wall, beneath a pipe holding up a row of shiny suits with flyaway lapels.

"I'm about to close up," she said. Then she added, as if I had begged her, "All right, maybe I can take a look."

Chuck opened and closed the trunk while I carried the stuff inside. He looked ready to bolt. His face was sickly white and he rolled his eyes like a spooked horse at the people moving past—derelicts, sailors, Indians in cowboy hats, winos doing their wino shuffle and shouting at enemies they alone could see. I was skittish myself. But it took more than a boy with his arms full of firepower to get the attention of these citizens. No one gave us a second look.

The pawnbroker ignored me as I went back and forth to the car. I lined everything up on the top of the cabinet and waited.

"That it?" she said.

I said that was it.

She came from around back and locked the door. Then she went behind the counter again. She ran her eyes over the goods. She picked up the double-barreled shotgun, broke it open, held the barrels up to the light and squinted through each of them in turn. Then she snapped the gun shut again, hard, too hard. It was painful to watch. I knew that gun, as I knew the other gun and the rifles. I had used them all and felt respect for them, and something more than respect. I did not like to see them handled as this woman handled them, slapping them around, levering and pumping the actions as if she were trying to break them. But I said nothing. I was unnerved by her big competent hands and her doll's face that never changed expression, and most of all by her refusal to look at me. The longer she didn't look at me the more I wanted her to. She made me feel insubstantial, which gave her the edge. And she knew what she was doing. She tore down every gun and rifle without hesitation, checked its barrel, checked its firing mechanism, and put it together again as fast as I could have.

Once she'd looked at them all she shrugged and said, "I don't need this truck."

"But you said you'd look at them."

She turned to the shelf behind her and started lifting things again. "I looked at them."

I stared at her back.

She said, "I might be able to take them as pawn."

"Pawn? How much can I pawn them for?"

She shrugged. "Five apiece."

"Five dollars? But that's not fair!"

She didn't answer.

"Your sign says you buy guns."

"I'm not buying any now."

"They're worth a lot more than that," I said. "A lot more."

"Then go get more."

"Maybe I will," I said, but I knew better now. I also knew that if Chuck saw me walk out the door with all these shooters in my hands he would leave without me. "I could sell them for twenty," I said.

"I already told you, I'm not buying. If you want to pawn, five's the limit." Then she said, "All right. Throw in those other whatnots and you got yourself a deal."

"You mean twenty apiece?"

She hesitated, then said, "Ten. Sixty for everything. Final offer."

"The binoculars are worth more than that," I said. "All by themselves."

"Not as pawn they aren't."

I kept staring at her back. She wasn't moving. She knew I was going to give in, I could feel her knowing it, and that made me determined not to give in. I picked up the shotguns. Then I put them down again. "Okay," I said.

She locked the door behind me when I left. The lock shot home with a smack. I dropped the pawn tickets in the gutter, just as she knew I would.

Amen

My father took off for Las Vegas with his girlfriend the day after I arrived in California. He left me with the keys to a rented Pontiac and a charge account at the corner grocery. For two weeks I drove back and forth along the beach and ate TV dinners and went to movies with an acquaintance of my father's who had offered to keep an eye on me. One morning I woke up to find this man embracing me and making declarations of love. I got him out of the apartment and called my father, who told me to "shoot the bastard" if he came back. For this purpose he directed me to a .223 Air Force Survival Rifle he had hidden in the closet. He waited on the telephone while I fetched the rifle from its hiding place, then instructed me in its assembly.

That night the man leaned against the apartment door and sobbed while I stood in the darkness on the other side, silently hugging the rifle, sweating and shaking as in a fever.

My father came home a few days before my brother arrived. He took me to meet Geoffrey's bus and dropped us both off at the apartment while he went out to buy some groceries for dinner. He didn't return. Several hours later his girlfriend called to say that he had gone crazy and was now in the custody of the police. My brother went down to the police station and confirmed that my father had indeed suffered some kind of breakdown. He committed him to Buena Vista Sanitarium, where, for the rest of the summer, my father played genial host to us on Sundays and became engaged to a series of women with even bigger problems than he had.

My mother saw which way the wind was blowing and declined to join us.

Geoffrey supported us all by working at Convair Astronautics. He had no time to write his novel, or even to prepare the classes he would be teaching in Istanbul that fall. While he worked I ran wild. He tried to keep me busy and get me ready for school by having me write essays on assigned reading. "Disease as Metaphor in *The Plague*." "Modes of Blindness in *Oedipus Rex*." "Conscience and Law in *Huckleberry Finn*." But he had better luck teaching me to love Django Reinhardt and Joe Venuti, and to sing, while he took tenor, the bass line in the glee-club songs he'd learned at Choate. We still sing them.

After I went East to school my mother took a job in Washington, D.C. During the Christmas holidays Dwight trailed her there and tried to strangle her in the lobby of our apartment building. Just before she blacked out she kneed him in the balls. He hollered and let her go; then he grabbed her purse and ran. While all this went on I was sitting in our room, reading *Hawaii* and languidly pretending to believe that the strange noises I heard came from cats. The neighborhood was rough, and I had formed the habit of assigning all such sounds to inhuman origin. When my mother stumbled upstairs and told me what had happened, I tore off blindly down the street and was immediately collared by a plainclothesman who suspected me of another crime. By the time I got home Dwight had been arrested. He was standing outside with my mother and two cops, staring at the ground, the lights of the cruiser flashing across his face.

"Bastard," I said, but I said it almost gently, conscious of the falseness of my position. I had known someone was in trouble and had done nothing.

Dwight raised his head. He seemed confused, as if he didn't recognize me. He lowered his head again. His curly hair glistened with melting snowflakes. This was my last sight of him. My mother got a cease-and-desist order, and the police put him on a bus for Seattle the next morning.

I DID NOT do well at Hill. How could I? I knew nothing. My ignorance was so profound that entire class periods would pass without my understanding anything that was said. The masters thought I was lazy, except for my English master, who saw that I loved books but had no way of talking about them beyond what I'd begun to learn from my brother. This man befriended me. He tutored me, cast me in some of the plays he directed, and tolerated the presumption his kindness sometimes gave rise to. But most of my teachers were clearly disappointed. It scared me to do so poorly when so much was expected, and to cover my fear I became one of the school wildmen—a drinker, a smoker, a make-out artist at the mixers we had with Baldwin and Shipley and Miss Fine's. But that's another story.

If I worked hard I could just stay afloat; as soon as I relaxed I went under. When I felt myself going under I panicked and did wildman things that got me in trouble. My demerit count was almost always the highest in the class. While the boys around me nodded off during Chapel I prayed like a Moslem, prayed that I would somehow pull myself up again so I could stay in this place that I secretly and deeply loved.

The school was patient, but not inexhaustibly patient. In my last year I broke the bank and was asked to leave. My mother met my train and took me to a piano bar full of men in Nehru jackets where she let me drink myself under the table. She wanted me to know that she wasn't mad about anything, that I'd lasted longer than she ever thought I would. She was in a mood to celebrate, having just landed a good job in the church across the street from the White House. "I've got a better view than Kennedy," she told me.

My best friend got kicked out of school a few weeks after me, and the two of us proceeded to rage. I wore myself out with raging. Then I went into the army. I did so with a sense of relief and homecoming. It was good to find myself back in the clear life of uniforms and ranks and weapons. It seemed to me when I got there that this was where I had been going all along, and where I might still redeem myself. All I needed was a war.

Careful what you pray for.

* * *

WHEN WE ARE green, still half-created, we believe that our dreams are rights, that the world is disposed to act in our best interests, and that falling and dying are for quitters. We live on the innocent and monstrous assurance that we alone, of all the people ever born, have a special arrangement whereby we will be allowed to stay green forever.

That assurance burns very bright at certain moments. It was burning bright for me when Chuck and I left Seattle and started the long drive home. I had just dumped a load of stolen goods. My wallet was thick with bills which I would lose at cards in one night, but which I then believed would keep me going for months. In a couple of weeks I was leaving for California to be with my father and my brother. Soon after I got there, my mother would join us. We would all be together again, as we were meant to be.

And when the summer was over I would go East to a noble school where I would earn good marks, captain the swimming team, and be welcomed into the great world that was my desire and my right. In this world nothing was impossible that I could imagine for myself. In this world the only task was to pick and choose.

Chuck felt good too. His trunk had no guns in it. He had escaped Tina Flood, he had escaped prison, and before long he would escape me. We weren't friends any more, but we both had cause to rejoice and this helped us imagine we were friends. We sang along with the radio and shared a bottle of Canadian Club

TOBIAS WOLFF

that Chuck had brought along. The deejay was playing songs from two and three years before, songs that already made us nostalgic. The farther we got from Seattle the louder we sang. We were rubes, after all, and for a rube the whole point of a trip to the city is the moment of leaving it, the moment it closes behind his back like a trap sprung too late.

The night was hazy. There was no moon. Farmhouse windows burned with a soft buttery light, as if they were under water. We went from farmland to forest and then picked up the river and followed the river into the mountains. I looked at the country we passed through with a lordly eye, allowing myself small stirrings of fondness for what I thought had failed to hold me. I did not know that the word *home* would forever after be filled with this place.

The air grew clearer as we climbed, and colder. The curves followed fast on one another as the road took the snaky shape of the river. We could see the moon now, a thin silver moon swinging between the black treetops overhead. Chuck kept losing the radio station. Finally he turned off the radio, and we sang Buddy Holly songs for a while. When we got tired of those, we sang hymns. First we sang "I Walk to the Garden Alone" and "The Old Rugged Cross," and a few other quiet ones, just to find our range and get in the spirit. Then we sang the roofraisers. We sang them with respect and we sang them hard, swaying from side to side and dipping our shoulders in counterpoint. Between hymns we drank from the bottle. Our voices were strong. It was a good night to sing and we sang for all we were worth, as if we'd been saved.